FEARLESS LEADERSHIP

FEARLESS
Leadership

Conquering Your Fears
And the Lies
That Drive Them

Bruce E. Roselle, PhD

 LEADER
PRESS
Minneapolis, Minnesota

LEADER PRESS is a registered trademark of Roselle Leadership Strategies, Inc., Minneapolis, MN. Communication should be directed to leaderpress@roselle-leadership.com. Visit the website www.roselleleadership.com for more information about publications from LEADER PRESS.

First printing, May 2006
Second printing, March 2008

Cover design: Amy Kirkpatrick, Kirkpatrick Design
Book design: Dorie McClelland, Spring Book Design

ISBN 13: 978-0-9785646-0-5

Library of Congress Catalog Number: 2006926202
Printed in the United States of America
10   09   08   6   5   4   3   2

To order, visit www.roselleleadership.com.

This book is dedicated to all those individuals who have shared their life stories, including their fears and the lies that drive them. I admire them for their courage and determination to live extraordinary lives.

CONTENTS

ACKNOWLEDGMENTS

As with most such projects, many people have contributed their thoughts and ideas to this book. First, I wish to thank the hundreds of managers and executives who have opened up their hearts and minds to me in the course of our coaching relationship. They have provided the rich details that bring these concepts alive and help to make them useful to you as the reader. These are the ones who have prepared the way for you by struggling to come to a deeper understanding of how anchor lies got in the way of their own effectiveness and success.

Several researchers and authors who have written earlier articles and books in this area contributed much to the conceptual framework of this book over the last 10 years. In the most fundamental way, I need to thank the founder of Cognitive Behavioral Therapy, Aaron Beck, who developed this approach in the 1970s. The basic tenets of cognitive behavioral theory are that people develop negative thinking patterns early in life based on irrational, dysfunctional beliefs and that these patterns can be identified and replaced with rational, functional beliefs. These changes in the underlying belief system then create positive changes in the person's behaviors and actions.

In an exhaustive 1988 review of the literature in the area of self-destructive tendencies, researchers Baumeister and Scher identified an area of research that supported the data I was collecting through my coaching interactions. The authors reviewed studies of "counterproductive strategies" in which individuals seek particular goals or outcomes, but are unsuccessful because they employ ineffective strategies and approaches. The authors conclude that self-defeating techniques are irrational in that they offer little in the way of benefit, yet people acquire, utilize, and maintain these patterns anyway. (Baumeister and Scher, "Self-Defeating Behavior Patterns Among Normal Individuals," *Psychological Bulletin* 104, 1988, 3–22.)

It was clear, then, that these patterns existed, but there was a great deal of uncertainty about how they are acquired in the first place. My friend Bob Hardy and his co-author Milton Cudney (*Self-Defeating Behaviors,* HarperSanFrancisco, 1991) successfully identified the underlying faulty conclusions and mythical fears that create self-defeating behaviors. Though the clinical stories they used to illustrate these concepts were somewhat removed from the executives I coached, the fundamental truths were applicable to my work. Their insights and examples in the book gave me a new, powerful direction for coaching and led to tremendous breakthroughs for my clients.

Years later, I was introduced to the work of Edward Smith. From his ground-breaking work with abuse victims, I gleaned the idea that we each hold on to a lie or set of lies about ourselves that originate in early childhood (*Healing Life's Deepest Hurts,* Vine Books, 2004). This concept substantiated my experiences in coaching and coincided nicely with the childhood origins discussed by Cudney and Hardy, and also with the findings of researcher and theorist Francine Shapiro. In the mid-1990s, Shapiro theorized that memory is stored in the brain via linked networks and organized around early life events and the feelings attached to them. Her model hypothesizes that when early life events are distressing or traumatic, the person's initial feelings and distorted thinking are stored in the brain just as they were experienced in the childhood events (*EMDR: the Breakthrough Therapy for Overcoming Anxiety, Stress, and Trauma,* New York: Basic Books, 1997). Based on a fusion of all these concepts, *Fearless Leadership* is illustrated with detailed stories and themes from my work as an executive coach.

Once the initial draft of this manuscript was written, some important people took time out of their busy lives to provide essential feedback on the content and flow. Several dear friends offered their time and energy to carefully go through each page and provide helpful suggestions. I am forever grateful to Dan Streeter and Irv Woolf for sacrificing a number of hours to carefully read these pages and for having the courage to provide some very specific comments. All of their comments and suggestions were incorporated in one way or another to strengthen the final manuscript. Ben Roselle and Kate Roselle proofread and edited the manuscript into its final, printed form.

Finally, I want to acknowledge my wife and life-partner,

Cindy, who was the first to edit and make comments on the book. It is difficult to be the first person to offer critical comments and to do it with compassion and grace—both of which my sensitive author heart needed! She has been steadfast and consistent in her love for me despite the lies and fears that have periodically exhibited their destructive behavior over our 30 years of marriage (and counting). Most importantly, she has had the courage to lovingly speak the truth to me about these, which has helped me become a better husband and father, a better listener and coach, and a more fearless leader in all aspects of my life.

FEARLESS LEADERSHIP

1

You Can't Always Get
What You Need

You've seen it happen in your workplace and have wondered to yourself, "What made him react that way; why is he being such a jerk?" Or you've been shopping in a store on a Saturday and overheard a mother lose her cool while trying vainly to pacify a belligerent child. Perhaps you have even caught yourself after a particularly defensive reaction to something your boss said to you, and have asked yourself later, "Where'd that come from?"

Each of these examples illustrates what happens when your buttons get pushed in a situation and then, suddenly, you react in a way that you hardly recognize. Knowing that your buttons got pushed and knowing why your buttons got pushed are two very different bits of knowledge. Maybe you have tried to explain why they got pushed by blaming the other person for how he or she delivered the message or what his or her underlying intentions were. The problem with blaming the person or situation is that you minimize the impact of your own actions and you fail to learn anything that could help you in the future.

REACTING VERSUS RESPONDING. Let's take a closer look at what it means to "get your buttons pushed." Usually what happens is that someone says or does something to you and you react immediately—much like you would if you touched a hot surface on your stove. In this kind of **reaction,** where the possibility of bodily harm exists, your central nervous system reflexively sends an electronic impulse to the hand/arm muscles to pull back sharply. This is the "reflex arc" that you probably learned about in secondary school science. The beauty of it is that this protective impulse does not take the time to go through the thought-producing cortex of your brain, but instead is handled in the lower brain.

The result is a swift and "thoughtless" reaction that protects your flesh from severe burns. In this kind of situation, with the possibility of real bodily danger, your brain protects you by short-circuiting your higher brain functions and moving quickly through the lower brain. In behavioral psychology terms, a stimulus—burning sensation—occurs, and you react by jerking your hand away involuntarily.

Similarly, when an object like a basketball, snowball, or fist suddenly appears in your peripheral vision, you involuntarily flinch. Like the reflex arc, this kind of quick reaction is also built into your lower brain functioning and it occurs without you purposely thinking, "Quick, pull your head to the side to avoid the flying object!" If you have ever been involved in a serious car accident, you have experienced a related phenomenon that occurs when adrenaline suddenly shoots through your body. Almost as if it is in slow motion, your body reacts by turning the wheel, stepping on the brake, or ducking your head, and at the same time your brain seems to have been shut off. No rational arguments, no logical treatises, no pro-con thinking occurs—only the muscles reacting to lower brain commands in a way that is designed to protect you from imminent harm.

How does this differ from "responding"? Generating a **response** to a person or situation around you involves taking in the information through your senses—sight, smell, touch, taste, hearing—and then considering this input within the thoughtful folds of your brain's cortex before speaking or acting. When you deliver a carefully considered response to a stimulus, you must draw upon your intellect, values, emotions, and previous experiences. Most of the decisions you make at work or at home are generated by this kind of considered response.

FEARLESS LEADERS. The most effective day-to-day responses you make are informed by your heart and your cortex working in concert with each other. This cannot happen when you are beset by fears and faulty beliefs that undermine your confidence and block your ability to think clearly. Fearless leaders approach their work with optimistic attitudes and embrace each new challenge with confidence and courage. They know the truth about themselves and are not stopped by their own irrational reactions. Leaders who are fearless in these ways use their hearts and minds together to create thoughtful, healthy responses to situations they face at every moment.

No matter what your title is, you are a leader in some aspect of your life. Whether you lead thousands, tens, or just yourself, it is important to do so at your maximum level of effectiveness. In your most high-performance mode, your actions reflect deeply-held beliefs and well-considered responses. When I ask leaders to describe themselves in this highly effective mode, they consistently use adjectives like:

- Decisive, action-oriented
- Confident and optimistic
- Focused and clear-thinking
- Collaborative, compassionate toward others

However, even the most effective leaders do not always function in a high-performance mode. Take Bill, for example. (Though Bill's story and other stories throughout this book are based on actual cases, the names have been changed, and in most cases the gender, type of organization, or functional area of the individual has also been altered.) Vice President of Operations for a large food products manufacturer, Bill was identified as a high potential individual and was on the fast track from the time he arrived six months earlier. He had been handed a couple of huge quality problems to fix in the manufacturing process, and had promptly and effectively acted to meet the challenge.

In just a few months, he developed the reputation as a bright guy who asked questions that cut to the core of issues, who quickly sized up his staff to determine who were the keepers and who needed to be replaced, and who pushed for results on a highly accelerated timetable. Bill's manager was clearly pleased with his energy and drive, as well as his ability to make difficult decisions without agonizing, procrastinating, or feeling guilty over them. Moreover, Bill had a warm smile, exhibited compassion for his coworkers, and was generally respected and admired.

After working with Bill for a few sessions aimed at fine-tuning his leadership skills, I began to wonder what he and I would actually work on. We talked through a couple of changes he intended to make in his group and a possible reorganization of his reporting relationships, but it didn't seem like we were destined to focus on anything with much substance. That's when he went off with his team for two days on a strategic retreat, and everything changed.

At the first day of the retreat, Bill facilitated the discussion and tried to nudge the group to take on some bigger challenges and to identify champions from the group who would take major responsibility. The more he pushed, the quieter and more unresponsive his team members became, until finally they sat silently. Bill was becoming increasingly agitated on the inside until it became too much for him, and in an instant, he shifted from an amiable Dr. Jekyll to a frustrated Mr. Hyde. Unable to contain himself any longer, he jumped up and began to angrily lecture the group and drive them toward the conclusions he desired. The day ended in chaos—a total fiasco that fell short of every one of Bill's objectives.

Thankfully, a couple human resource partners were also present at this strategic retreat, and they talked about it with Bill over dinner and into the night. Among the three of them, they came up with an alternative strategy for the second day of the retreat. That day, they managed to salvage a couple of the major objectives of the retreat and people left feeling that they had accomplished something—but not without paying a high price.

Bill was left wondering who had taken over his body and run amok in front of the group. It was at this point in the coaching that I introduced the concepts from this book, and helped him recognize how his behavior on the afternoon of the first day was a clear example of his reacting rather than responding effectively to a difficult situation. Without warning he had shifted into his reactive mode, and to those present, it probably looked like something from *Invasion of the Body Snatchers*. After that retreat, Bill and I suddenly had plenty to work on and I had his full attention in the coaching sessions.

In a very different way, Julie illustrates a similar irrational set of behaviors that pop out when she and others least expect them. The president of a medium-sized advertising firm, Julie has a reputation in the firm and in the local industry as being smart and competitive. Gracious, charming, and strategic, she has the ability to energize people with her creative vision and a personal style that is powerfully effective. When she facilitates discussion with her senior team and with clients, she has the ability to move them emotionally and intellectually.

One of the members of her core leadership group—a VP/ Account Supervisor named David—was given the assignment to find ways to include Julie in high-level client contacts so that her presence would help make the sale in new business pitches. For several months, Julie and David had discussed a strategy for introducing her to the top executives of their key clients, but somehow the connections never happened. Though they disagreed on what caused this problem, the net result was that these high level meetings had not occurred and both were getting frustrated with what they each perceived as a lack of intentional action on the part of the other.

One night, Julie was invited to take part in a charity ball sponsored by one of their key clients. She decided to bring David with her as her escort, and as someone who could finally introduce her to this major client and others that would likely be in attendance at this gala event. As the evening progressed, however, Julie seemed to get shy about actually launching into small talk with the several key clients who were present, and David became increasingly frustrated with what he perceived as Julie's resistance to making these high level contacts.

Neither one spoke of his or her agitation to the other, but in the car on the way back to the office, Julie unloaded her frustration on David and accused him of blocking her from making these contacts and deliberately undermining her ability to personally connect with them. For his part, David felt totally blindsided by this angry, personal attack and wondered whether he and his boss would ever be able to work together on client initiatives. David felt that Julie's outburst was an extreme overreaction that stemmed from her inability to fully trust him or depend on him to do his job. The net result was an evening that was a fiasco and a working relationship that was severely burned.

Where do these out-of-character, unproductive reactions come from? Why do they persist even though, like Bill and Julie, we can clearly see that they get in the way of our immediate objectives as well as our overall effectiveness? They persist because we each have some very deep and fundamental needs that do not always feel as if they are being fulfilled in our lives. In our sometimes clumsy attempts to meet those needs, we occasionally engage in behaviors that become obstacles to our effectiveness.

OUR MOST IMPORTANT NEEDS. As human beings, we have several fundamental needs that must be met in order for us to feel fulfilled. When you think of needs that you have in your day-to-day life, you might list such things as being respected, receiving forgiveness from others, knowing that you are under-stood by people, or feeling appreciated by your coworkers. All of these are important needs, and we could probably name tens or hundreds of other specific needs that you have throughout the month or year. With each of the specific needs you identify, you might ask yourself why this need exists in you. For example, "Why do I need to be forgiven by my friend?" or "Why is the respect of my peers so important to me?" are questions that can lead to a deeper understanding of yourself.

If you were to engage in this kind of soul-searching, it might lead you to a deeper level of understanding and a conclusion such as, "because I need to feel like people like me and accept me for who I am." Being liked and accepted lies at the core of most people's needs in life. In fact, the three most basic needs can be thought of as:

- Respect,
- Acceptance,
- Security.

We need to know that we are respected—important, significant, valued, worthy—in our work and in our relationships. We need to feel accepted in these areas as well—to know that we are liked, loved, and included. Finally, we need to know that we will be secure from emotional, physical, financial, or interpersonal harm.

Because these needs are not perfectly fulfilled in every moment, we live our lives each day falling short of complete satisfaction. The more we feel a lack of fulfillment of these basic needs and a hollow satisfaction, the greater the anxiety we experience and the more driven we are to fill the anxious space inside us. When our need for respect is particularly strong, we seem to be imploring others with words and actions that call out, *"Don't overlook me or ignore me—but instead, notice me and value me!"* Alternatively, when the need for acceptance has gone unfulfilled for a while, our behaviors and conversation speak loudly, *"Don't leave me—but instead stay with me, focus on me!"* When the need for security is strong, we communicate it to others in ways that say, *"Don't hurt me or let me be hurt—protect and look out for me!"*

Though we can talk about these needs and understand them in our conscious minds, they are mostly unconscious as they motivate our behavior. In Bill's case, his strong need to be valued created a great deal of pressure to perform as a superstar. By the afternoon of that first day of the strategic retreat, he was convinced that his group was not committed or competent enough to respond to the challenges that faced them. At the same time, below the radar of his cortex, he began to worry that he would never get this group where it needed to be for him to live up to his manager's and his own expectations. With Julie, her unexpressed need to be respected and secure in her relationships with key agency clients drove her to over-react and blame her direct report, David.

As we will discover in the next chapters, the stuff that lies below the radar of your cortex can be thought of as **anchor lies** and **irrational fears.** To put it simply, when at some unconscious level you begin to worry that your most fundamental needs of respect, acceptance, or security will not be met, it stirs up an irrational fear in you. When that fear instantaneously connects with a **faulty belief** in your subconscious mind, you begin to behave in a way that can best be characterized as a thoughtless reaction, or a "retroaction."

We refer to those connections of irrational fear and faulty belief as **retroactions** because they are reflexive behaviors you exhibit in the present, but are actually rooted to some occurrence or series of occurrences from your past. These automatic reactions echo fears and faulty beliefs from your early childhood and, in some ways, represent a regression to more childish behavior. Retroactions are intended to protect you from the irrational fear, but instead they usually hurt you by making your thoughtless reactions even more obvious to the people around you.

Why do these retroactions stick with us and continue to generate thoughtless reactions over the course of our lives? Because they are held fast by an anchor lie that we subconsciously believe to be true about ourselves. Here's how the connection to the past happens:

- A current event occurs.

- Association is made in our subconscious mind with an upsetting memory event from childhood.

- Untrue statements (anchor lies) about ourselves from the memory event stir up irrational fears inside us.

- The irrational fears connect with one or more faulty beliefs.

- These fears and faulty beliefs are immediately transferred to the present situation.

- We react thoughtlessly, and others around us see our retroactions.

Confused by this quick overview? The next chapters break this model down into understandable pieces and illustrate each with stories and anecdotes to help you recognize your own retroactions and become more effective in your life. The purpose of this book is to help you fully understand the role of anchor lies, irrational fears, and faulty beliefs in making you stumble in thoughtless reaction to situations, and then to provide some strategies so that you can catch yourself and shift to a more highly effective response.

REFLECTION MOMENT—QUESTIONS TO CONSIDER

Take some time now to thoughtfully consider your answers to these questions, and capture them here or write them on a separate sheet of paper. You can use your responses to focus your thinking and to share with others in a discussion group based on this book.

1. In which situations in your work and non-work lives do you have a tendency to react thoughtlessly (retroact) rather than respond effectively? What seems to "set you off" most often in these situations?

2. When you are responding to people and situations in your best, most effective, high performance mode, how would you describe the way you feel on the inside, as well as how you might come across to others?

3. In which settings and relationships in your life do your needs for respect, acceptance, and security feel the most fulfilled? When do they feel least fulfilled?

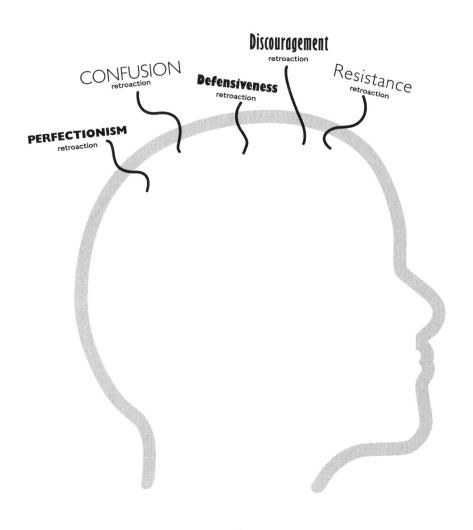

2

One Step Forward, Two Steps Back

Several years ago, I met an old friend and another guy for an afternoon of golf followed by dinner at a nearby restaurant. It had been a number of years since I had gotten together with my friend, and I had been looking forward to the conversation more than the golf. The other guy who tagged along that afternoon and evening was someone I had met briefly a couple of decades earlier and with whom I had completely lost contact. I was excited about the prospect of using our dinner conversation to get to know them again.

The golfing was painful but expected, based on how little skill the three of us possessed and how infrequently we played the game. Dinner was a relief from the reality of our play on the course, so we settled in to a booth and ordered. After we had caught up a bit in our lives with the more surface stuff and had consumed a good deal of the food on our plates, I decided to open up the discussion to other topics. So, I asked something like, "How do you know what to believe?" My intent was to initiate some philosophical and spiritual conversation and take things into interesting waters. It worked, and we were off on a lively and, at times, strained discussion and debate.

Just before we drained the last cup of coffee and polished off dessert, my friend's friend—who we will call Zach—was talking in a fairly negative way about some aspects of religion and faith. As I followed them out the door and into the empty parking lot, I said something like, "Zach, I know how you feel because I used to think about these things just like you do." Before these words were completely out of my mouth, Zach spun on his heel to face me, and I could see that his face was contorted with anger. In that moment, he spewed out the words, "You can't even begin to know me—you think that spending a couple of hours with me gives you the right to say you know me?!" His voice was so disdainful and angry, that I fully expected to see green slime froth out of his mouth like in the Exorcist movie. I froze, took a step backward and said a brief prayer about what to say next.

Before I could think it through, my mouth began to speak. The words I haltingly spoke went something like this, "Zach, I can see from your reaction that I must have said something that was very upsetting to you, and I apologize for whatever it was I said. Help me understand what I did or said that made you so angry." Then I paused and wondered what might come out of him next. I didn't need to wait long to find out.

What followed was about 15 stressful minutes of angry rhetoric and responses to my calm questioning and demeanor. My goal was to ride this tsunami wave of upset until it ran out of surge, and to avoid getting hurt in the process. Zach continued to rant and verbally attack and I listened and apologized where it felt appropriate. Occasionally, I appealed to my friend—who thankfully was still present—to clarify or confirm things that I had or had not said in the restaurant. After a very emotionally draining period of time, Zach's face suddenly relaxed and he let out a deep sigh. He paused a moment, and then turned to me somewhat sheepishly to apologize for his attack and to explain that, "I've been working on that rage thing." In my psychologist mind at that moment, it was clear that Zach's "rage thing" needed a lot more work, but I quickly determined not to make that suggestion.

The story of Zach at the restaurant, while perhaps more dramatic than most you will personally encounter, provides a powerful illustration of what occurs when the anchor lies and fears we introduced in the last chapter become aroused. As Zach probably could attest from his work on his rage, you often make progress one day and then fall back again the next. In your own life, do you ever get the feeling that as you try to become more effective in an area of behavior, you tend to fall backward two steps for each step forward?

The truth is that habitual behaviors like Zach's are very difficult to change. This is especially true if you're trying to change them at the level of the action itself, rather than through a deeper understanding of the causal dynamics. That is, you can make checklists of behaviors you desire to remove from your repertoire and speak affirmations to yourself about new behaviors you are trying to adopt, but these will have little impact unless you understand why you developed the undesirable behaviors in the first place, as well as what keeps them in place.

So, how do you avoid this typical "one step forward, two steps back" failure pattern in trying to change your behaviors? First, by recognizing that the patterns of your current behavior began very early in your life and that they have become ingrained. This is a good thing if we are talking about habits like listening without interrupting, responding compassionately to people who are upset, or taking an assertive stand when others around you suggest a dishonest approach. But what about habits that represent thoughtless reactions to people and situations—ones that cause harm to others or to you? These are problematic behaviors that we might want to change, but we are typically not fully aware of what they are and how they negatively impact others.

These thoughtless reactions and our ability to recognize them have something in common with a simple card game I learned as a child. In this game, each person picks a card and, without looking at it, holds it to his or her forehead facing out so everyone else can see it. No one in this game actually knows what value appears on his or her own card, but can only read what is on every other person's card. You must guess what is on your own card by reading the expression on other people's faces.

This game is a good metaphor for life, for we never are able to see ourselves "real time" as others around us see us. When they are aroused by a situation outside of you, your irrational fears and faulty beliefs are not directly observable because they exist only deep inside your brain. We never really know if the look on our face matches our message or tone of voice. And we cannot truly understand how our own behaviors come across and are interpreted by others. Fortunately, there is some consistency in how we react when in the throes of our retroactions and it is possible to recognize them from the inside, with some insight and a little practice. Even though most of these behaviors occur outside of our consciousness, we are often aware of small portions of them. We are conscious, for example, of how it feels on the inside when our irrational fears become stirred up. Oftentimes, we become aware of how others react to our behavior, much like in my description of the childhood card game.

The externally visible behaviors that signal the existence of your **retroactions** can be thought of as clustering into five distinct "card faces":

> **Confusion:** becoming suddenly uncertain about a decision or action; "doe in the headlights."

> **Perfectionism:** being driven by impossibly high standards, and expecting to hit goals every time.

> **Defensiveness:** perceiving the need to protect oneself, tending to take personally things that others say.

> **Resistance:** avoiding the control of others, responding with either passivity or aggression to keep them away.

> **Discouragement:** being overwhelmed with the difficulty of a goal; feeling pessimistic, hopeless, without energy.

When you observe these kinds of thoughtless reactions in yourself or others, they usually signal the existence of your underlying irrational fears. If you think of them in terms of how you feel on the inside, here are some combinations of retroactions and typical emotions:

- *Anger*—often caused by feeling attacked and trying to protect yourself **(defensiveness)**, trying to drive others away so they cannot control you **(resistance)**, or believing you will not perfectly achieve your or others' expectations **(perfectionism)**.

- *Anxiety*—usually caused by not being able to think clearly **(confusion)**, feeling overwhelmed by the difficulty of a task **(discouragement)**, or worrying that things will not be up to expected standards **(perfectionism)**.

- *Frustration*—most typically caused by setting expectations too high and recognizing that you are not likely to deliver on them **(perfectionism)**.

- *Uncertainty*—often paired with sudden lack of confidence in a decision **(confusion)**, feeling overwhelmed with the difficulty of an initiative **(discouragement)**, or trying to find the best solution to a problem **(perfectionism)**.

Let's look more closely at each of the five retroactions.

CONFUSION. Confusion becomes apparent as a retroaction when you see it in someone who normally is confident and assertive about a decision or action. In this mode, one appears to become suddenly stupid—to need much more structure and support than usual, or to exhibit that "doe in the headlights" look. When this happens, the response of others is typically to begin to reassure the individual, or to add structure and direction in order to "shore the person up."

Often when you try to help a suddenly confused individual, however, you get a response that indicates the person recognizes you are offering help but that your ideas will not help. This sort of response provides a glimpse of the irrational fear lying just underneath the surface. When people are truly confused and looking for clarification, they do not typically resist a helpful suggestion with a "yes, but" response. But when that confusion is the result of a fear becoming stirred up, and a faulty belief and lie being unconsciously engaged, you will see resistance or defensiveness to your attempts to help.

Confusion is one of the retroactions that others who know me well may see on my face from time to time. It usually happens when I am not sure I can do a particular thing or when I really do not want to do a specific task. Though I am typically seen as a quick problem solver, I am suddenly unable to think my way through an issue or task. It might be something that appears from the outside to be as simple as adding oil to a gas-powered engine or something as seemingly complex as determining the flow of a leadership workshop. Whatever the situation, when I become "suddenly stupid" and unable to think my way through a problem, I know that there is something about the situation and the issues attached to it that have stirred up an irrational fear in me.

Also suffering from confusion is Henry, the controller for a rapidly expanding manufacturer of winter sports equipment. He grew up living on a resort where his parents were part-time caretakers and worked in other professions the rest of the week. His parents were always busy, always involved in a project or two, and they instilled in him the importance of working until the job is done and not engaging in idle time. Henry became quite proficient at a wide array of athletic and construction-related skills, but despite these capabilities, his mother was very hard on him as the oldest child. Having become pregnant with Henry during her first semester of college, she was resentful of him and blamed him for her unhappiness and sense of failure in her life. Consequently, Henry developed the mindset that he always needed to expect more from himself and that nothing he ever did would be great or perfect.

Beginning to think of himself as not very capable of making good decisions in his work as an adult, Henry developed a habit of getting very confused about which direction to go related to the company's finances. Believing that he must always make the right choice, he began to pull back from decisions, hesitating, and analyzing them to death until others became very frustrated with his hesitance and inability to move on a decision. Because he also felt that he should be the financial expert most of the time, he rebuffed help that his boss and others might offer, and instead hunkered down to "figure it out on my own." Most of the time, the harder Henry pulled away to think about it, the more confused he became trying to come up with the right decision—and the more frustrated and annoyed others became with him.

PERFECTIONISM. The basis of perfectionism is being driven by impossibly high standards, which then impacts the ability to function effectively. It is great to have high standards and ideals, but it is critically important to recognize that most of the time our output will fall short in some way from the ideal we have in mind. Though an individual's performance is generally enhanced by some amount of arousal or tension, too much tension or anxiety will have a negative impact on performance output.

Perfectionism takes on two very different appearances. In some cases, people procrastinate and put things off until there is not enough time to deliver at the impossibly high standard they have set for themselves. They become paralyzed in the interest of thoroughly analyzing the problem and determining the optimal solution, and in thinking through the various possibilities to arrive at the perfect outcome. Procrastination thus provides a "safety valve" for their perfectionism. In other cases, people overcommit in their desire to always be responsive to others' needs, and then must become rigidly controlling in order to deliver at the highest standard all they have promised. With their procrastinating and highly controlling behaviors, perfectionists are difficult to collaborate with and not much fun to be around.

One might assume that most perfectionists became that way due to parents and influential adult role models who set specific and unrealistically high standards for them as children. This is certainly true in some of the people with whom I have worked over the years. But a more powerful influence on perfectionism seems to be parents and early authority figures who are generally demanding and critical, but who are also very unclear and non-specific about the results they expect. This latter situation sets up a fear of being criticized for not achieving results, but not being sure what the desired results are that would please parents. One individual I coached described it as, "not knowing if I have set the bar high enough, and believing that I must continually set it higher." This combination appears to create the maximum amount of perfectionism and stress in people.

This was certainly the case with Trent, the VP of Strategic Business Development for a major commercial construction firm. Describing himself as "an insecure overachiever with a need to be perfect," he typically tried to prove himself throughout his career by working harder than anyone else because he did not think of himself as very bright. He grew up with an alcoholic father who "checked out" at night after a few drinks, and did not communicate with Trent or the rest of the family. Since he either heard no feedback from his dad, or heard his opinions influenced by the liquor, Trent never trusted what his father said about him. Instead, in the absence of any meaningful feedback, he decided to try to be whoever people around him seemed to want him to be—especially to be highly competent and likable so that people would accept him.

He believed that he needed to always over-deliver on results and to add value in whatever he accomplished. Sometimes, the stress he experienced was nearly paralyzing when he was not prepared, did not have a ready answer to someone's question, or overlooked an important piece of data. In spite of all his accomplishments and positive feedback from his boss and others, he persisted in thinking that his work was nothing special and that he could lose his job at any time.

In a way similar to Trent, Naomi tended to overlook or not hear positive feedback from others as she strived to deliver perfect results in her role as Creative Director for a large art and photography gallery. Her job required her to work closely with a number of artists and photographers who displayed work in the gallery, as well as to coordinate a number of volunteer tour guides. Complicating her work situation was a boss who expected a very high level of excellence in Naomi's work, but who gave very little direction to her in advance. This left Naomi with her own and her boss's very high standards, but with little or no feedback on whether or not she had achieved them.

This combination of high standards and low feedback is the standard alchemy for perfectionistic behavior. Naomi grew up in a family with two older sisters and parents who were usually expressive in their love. However, when it was time for her to head off to Kindergarten for the first time, she quickly developed school phobic behavior in which she felt sick and upset and wanted to go back home. She often sat crying in her teacher's lap and just wanting to leave school for the comfort of Mom and Dad. After her first traumatic year of transitioning to school, Naomi was mostly an average student who needed help with homework at night. The only subject she clearly excelled in was anything related to Art. She recalls being terrified of being called on or asked to go up to the blackboard in front of the class, where she might feel embarrassed or humiliated. Her fear was that she would not know the right answer, and the teacher and her classmates would laugh at her or think she was stupid.

Out of these early school experiences, Naomi became a perfectionist who held herself to impossibly high standards, even though her parents and others encouraged her to lighten up and relax about school. Afraid that others would reject her and not like her if she did not perform at the top all the time, she developed the idea that if she was always in control of things, she would not suffer embarrassment at poor results. She began to tell herself things such as, "I need to think things through and be totally prepared, or I won't make the right decision," or "If I were to say no to this request, that would be totally unacceptable." From these beliefs and fears developed a controlling, perfectionistic behavior that was hard on Naomi and hard on all the people who worked for her and around her.

DEFENSIVENESS. In many ways, defensiveness is the "universal donor" among the retroactions because so many of us become defensive so readily when our underlying fears get agitated by people and circumstances. Defensiveness has many facets, each of which is designed to protect us from a perceived personal threat. In some cases, people become arrogant as a way of protecting themselves, believing that the best defense is an offense. Other people become suspicious and hyper-vigilant in order to protect themselves from any hint of a threat from others. Still others become "prickly" with argumentativeness and abrasiveness in order to keep people at arm's length, or they joke inappropriately to distract others from uncomfortable topics. The common thread in each of these descriptions is the irrational need to protect oneself from people and situations that, in fact, are not dangerous or threatening.

Marilyn, a young and aggressive marketing director for a manufacturer of computer hardware, provides a clear illustration of the suspicious/hyper-vigilant facet of defensiveness. Most of our coaching focused on helping her generate interpretations of the actions of her manager and peers that were not based on a defensive fear. She so totally distrusted one peer in particular that she constantly strategized a counter offensive to protect herself. Though less intensely protective with the rest of her peers, Marilyn was extremely hyper-vigilant around her boss. This made her interactions with him very hesitant and tenuous, or on the other extreme, angry and attacking. There was very little middle ground with Marilyn, for in this space she would need to drop her guard a bit and leave herself vulnerable.

Perhaps the most dramatic illustration of arrogant defensiveness occurred when I provided one executive, Warren, with some anecdotal feedback from his peers. As I summarized people's comments, his face began to contort and his eyes began to narrow. Before several minutes had elapsed, Warren's mouth opened up and out of it spewed some of the most angry, condescending, and arrogant comments about other people that I had ever heard. Since most of the feedback I had given him was focused on his arrogant, condescending, and abrasive style, I suddenly understood what others were seeing in Warren that made him so difficult to work with.

As Warren wrapped up his vitriolic diatribe, I began to smile and then to chuckle. Just as he was about to turn his anger on me, I remarked, "This was great for me to watch your reaction— now I really understand what they see in you that puts them off!" He looked at me with total lack of comprehension. Because his reaction was based on unconscious, irrational fears and habitual responses, he was also "unconscious" to how caustic his responses were and how negatively people reacted to them. Both the written feedback and my impromptu comments took his conscious mind totally by surprise. From this strong dose of reality, we were able to begin coaching that focused on where his irrational fears came from and how to employ more effective communication strategies and techniques.

RESISTANCE. Resistance is based on the irrational belief that control by others must be avoided at all costs. Closely connected are the underlying beliefs that "people cannot be trusted and that I must rely on myself for protection." Like perfectionism, resistance tends to have a couple distinct facets that shift from passive to aggressive. One facet of resistance is the tendency to passively avoid the control of others by simply ignoring their requests or avoiding them so that they cannot make the requests or follow through. This includes

- *Silent disagreements*—not agreeing but not communicating the disagreement,

- *False compliance*—agreeing publicly but disagreeing privately, and

- *Undermining*—stirring up discontent behind the scenes.

A second facet of resistance features an aggressive, attacking style of putting people off so that they cannot exert any control. These people are viewed by others as bullies, and exhibit behaviors that include:

- *Threatening people* with losing their jobs or with other sanctions if they do not get in line.
- *Responding with hostility* to any criticisms, suggestions, or assertive statements.

One of my favorite stories of the more passive type of resistance defined above was my own attempt to resist the control of a former boss. While employed as a senior staff psychologist at a major Midwestern university, I reported to a person whom I did not trust. The distrust began during the interview process, built during our salary negotiations, and only increased after I began to work for her. We met every week for an individual meeting and it became clear to me very early on that she used these meetings to hammer home her agenda, with little discussion about what I hoped to accomplish in my role. Each time we met, I left her office with a longer list of tasks she wanted me to complete— ones that took me further from my own list of priorities.

After several months, however, I began to recognize a pattern in my boss's work week. She often attended regional and national conferences as part of her role, and typically was out of the office on Fridays. At the time, our meetings were scheduled for Mondays and she was in the office on this day nearly every week. Trying not to arouse any suspicions on her part, I requested that we change our meetings to Fridays. She agreed, but requested that I contact her secretary to set alternative times if either of us could not make the meetings. I agreed, but never actually took steps to reschedule our meetings. Since she was out of the office almost every other week, I figured I had cut my extra projects in half for the rest of my tenure there. Though I am not proud of it, this example clearly illustrates an avoiding, false compliance type of resistance.

The hostile, attacking style of resistance is depicted by Trevor, Chief Financial Officer for a large insurance and financial services organization. My first introduction to Trevor was through a couple of his peers on the senior management team who specifically noted his attacking style when I interviewed them about the strengths and development needs of their team. They described him as a Pit Bull who got his jaws around a particular position on an issue and then would not let go. If others put up a fight, he would attack their logic and facts, and often, he would attack them personally. After several years of this kind of abuse, most members of the senior team had given up the fight and simply waited silently with the hope that the president would step in and "call him off" on an issue.

Once I got to know Trevor better in the context of feedback and coaching, it became clear that he was a bright and verbal financial guy who had a loving family and was seen by them and his friends as a very nice person. The problem was that when he got involved with major decisions for the company—decisions on which he viewed himself as the financial gatekeeper—his underlying fears of getting hurt financially got stirred up. As this happened, his irrational belief was that he must wrestle control from his peers, and sometimes from his boss, in order to protect his "investment" in the company. From the outside, however, this retroaction mostly looked like hostile resistance to being influenced or controlled by others.

DISCOURAGEMENT. The primary influence here is that the person becomes totally overwhelmed with the enormity and perceived difficulty of a particular goal. On the inside, the discouraged individual will often feel a low level of confidence and motivation to move forward. Discouraged people tend to worry about potential outcomes and be pessimistic about possibilities. On the outside, they often appear overwhelmed and exhibit a low energy level. This phenomenon is distinct from clinical depression, which typically lasts for months or years, and in its bipolar version is paired with manic periods. Discouragement is a retroaction to a particular situation by an otherwise highly functioning individual.

Perhaps an example will help paint the picture. Janet runs her own small business as an area franchise developer and franchise owner. Other franchise owners and people in the corporate development office describe her as bright and analytical, effective with details, and holding to very high standards. People also see her as a bit rigid and intense at times, but overall a very strong franchise developer and leader. In talking with her, however, I discovered that she often experienced periods of intense discouragement that blocked her from effectively handling a problem or task. A great deal of what motivated her at work was to take on new challenges. She had, in fact, created the franchise development function from nothing, and prior to going off on her own had developed a marketing function for this company where none had previously existed.

Though Janet was strongly motivated to take on challenges, she also periodically became overwhelmed in attempting to overcome the challenging problems she took on. This is when the discouragement would set in. Through our coaching, she began to recognize that her significance as a person was not determined by whether or not she had delivered on some difficult task today. Eventually, Janet was able to see the difference between being disappointed about an objective not fully achieved, and being overwhelmed and discouraged by an irrational sense of personal failure and a belief that she was fundamentally inadequate.

Sometimes, it is very difficult to determine where the fears and faulty beliefs get started in a person. Such is the case with Paul, Marketing Director for a large food products manufacturer, who grew up in a family of three siblings in a small town where he was always surrounded by parents and extended family members. He described his mom as quite expressive of her love using words, while his dad tended to convey his love through his actions toward Paul. The second oldest, Paul grew up fairly independently because his parents always treated him as someone more mature than his actual age. Usually a bit better in school than his older brother, Paul was also a very good athlete, especially in football. He was recognized for his prowess and tended to be very confident in his athletic and academic abilities.

At some point in his early life, however, Paul started to

become more guarded and self-conscious. He could not pull any specific events from memory that might have had a dramatic effect on this behavior, but clearly recognized that it was getting in the way of his effectiveness as an adult. What usually happened to stir up these fears is that, as Paul was trying to communicate with his boss or other senior people in the organization, he would begin to think, "I don't know these people that well, and they don't know me, so I must do something to drive things to a new level, or they will question my competence." With every action he took that was visible to higher management, he felt that somehow his credibility and job were on the line, and that if he was unable to figure things out in a way that had high impact, he might just as well "throw in the towel." This kind of retroaction often led to Paul feeling overwhelmed and discouraged about ever making a big enough difference to be seen as competent.

As a quick reminder, the five retroactions we have been addressing include the following:

Confusion: becoming suddenly uncertain about a decision or action; "doe in the headlights."

Perfectionism: being driven by impossibly high standards, and expecting to hit goals every time.

Defensiveness: perceiving the need to protect oneself, tending to take personally things that others say.

Resistance: avoiding the control of others, responding with either passivity or aggression to keep them away.

Discouragement: being overwhelmed with the difficulty of a goal; feeling pessimistic, hopeless, without energy.

As we have discussed, they represent the "faces" of our thoughtless reactions—the part we can visibly observe in others and they can see in us, but we often have difficulty recognizing in ourselves. We need to get under the surface, however, to really understand how these retroactions occur and then begin to develop a strategy for how to reduce or eliminate them in our lives. Typically, the first part of the chain reaction is an event from the present that stirs up irrational fears from the past. This is the focus of the next chapter.

REFLECTION MOMENT—QUESTIONS TO CONSIDER

Take some time now to thoughtfully consider your answers to these questions, and capture them here or write them on a separate sheet of paper. You can use your responses to focus your thinking and to share with others in a discussion group based on this book.

1. **In what situations in your daily life do you tend to overreact and become upset?**

2. **Which of the five retroactions (confusion, perfectionism, defensiveness, resistance, or discouragement) do you most commonly exhibit when your buttons are pushed? What does it look like and feel like inside you?**

3. **Which other retroactions do you recognize as ones you use? Which story in this chapter of people like Zach, Naomi, Paul, Trent, Marilyn, etc. seemed to hit home the most with you or was most like you?**

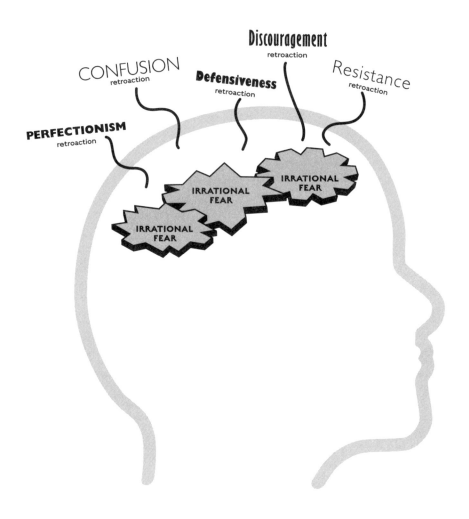

3

Under the Influence of Fear

As we have discussed, the most fundamental needs we have
as human beings are acceptance, respect, and security. When
these needs are threatened in some way in the present, our lower
brains make an immediate connection to subconscious, irrational fears from the past. Like barnacles on the hull of a sleek
ship, these fears attach themselves to the fundamental needs and
make it difficult to live and lead fearlessly. We begin to ask ourselves questions such as, "What if people don't like or accept me?
What if my boss demotes me or takes me off the decision-making team? What if I lose my job altogether—how will I support
my family?" Unlike the fundamental needs, which are rational
and for the most part conscious, these fears are mostly irrational
and unconscious. Consequently, they are difficult to identify
and highly resistant to change.

Most of us have some fears of which we are consciously
aware. They include things like public speaking, failing in a visible project, looking stupid, becoming embarrassed, and being

taken advantage of. These are the kinds of fears that we know are present in our minds, and may even have discussed with others we trust. But there are deeper fears than these. You can confirm this by asking yourself why you are afraid, for example, of failing or losing at something. Once you get past the surface response of "just because," you will begin to realize that there is another level of fear underneath these fears. When you ask yourself, "So what if I fail (or look stupid, or get embarrassed, etc.)?" you recognize that there is an answer rooted somewhere deeper in your psyche.

When I play this "so what" game with people and pose this kind of question, they often respond with "If I fail at a work project, others will not trust my competence." A follow-up question such as, "So what if they don't trust your competence?" will eventually lead to another level of fear. The answers here are typically issues like, "They will not accept me as a peer," or "They will remove me from the team or demote me," or "They will fire me." At this level, the answers often highlight one or more of the three most fundamental **irrational fears:**

> **Personal rejection.** People will not like me, accept me, or include me.

> **Role insignificance.** Others in authority will not look to me, value me, or allow me to play an important role.

> **Irreparable hurt.** The situation will shift dramatically and people important to me or I, myself, will be damaged emotionally, financially, or physically in a way that cannot be repaired.

These are the three most basic fears we face every day, and they are irrational because they are typically not attached to real dangers or threats in our environment. Irrational fears are those that become attached in illogical ways to objects that might not otherwise be fearful. In real, rational fear situations—like automobile accidents, grizzly bear encounters, or theft at gunpoint—we typically do not feel the effects of the fear until after the event. As a response to these kinds of situations, our adrenaline kicks in and our bodily responses take over in the actual moment. Everything seems to happen in slow motion. It is not until after the event that our heart beats wildly, our knees turn to rubber, and we feel faint.

In real fear situations, then, we normally feel the bulk of the fear *after* the event. With the irrational fears of rejection, insignificance, and hurt, however, we typically feel the effects of the fear *before* the event actually occurs. We worry about it in advance, we "psych ourselves out," and we lose sleep or appetite as the event approaches. These are all examples of the effects of irrational fear.

These irrational fears are, in effect, mirror images of our most fundamental needs. Our need for acceptance is threatened by our fear of rejection, our need for respect is put into jeopardy by our fear of insignificance, and our need for security is compromised by our fear of getting hurt. Because they so fundamentally undermine our sense of well-being, these three irrational fears are capable of motivating our behavior in very powerful ways. To further complicate matters, these fears are almost completely unconscious, which is why it takes something like a series of "so what" questions described above to get down to them.

While many theorists, scientists, and practitioners in the area of irrational fear agree that their effects are powerful and highly motivating, there is not full agreement on the question of where the fears reside in the brain. Some draw a distinction between the conscious mind and the preconscious or unconscious mind. In this dichotomy, the **cortex** is considered the higher brain in which logical analysis, creative problem solving, memory, and other complicated conscious functions operate. This framework suggests that the foundations of our irrational fears are embedded in the lower brain or **limbic system.** Unlike the cortex, these lower brain components—ones that are located between the cortex and the brain stem—store memories that are primarily emotional in nature.

Others in this field put greater emphasis on the distinction between left and right hemispheric functioning in the brain. From their perspective, the left brain is the place where language, reasoning, information, and autobiographical memory are stored, while the right brain contains emotional memories, feelings, and a control center that determines our emotional responses to situations. More important to these theorists than the upper/lower brain distinction is the synchronization between the right brain's emotional memories and the left brain's words that explain these feelings. In this framework, the retroactions start to occur when our left brain explanations and information do not fit with our right brain experiences and feelings. Some scientists think of the brain as hierarchical layers, others as coexisting modules.

Most of the authorities agree on one thing, however: early childhood wounds of varying degrees of severity tend to create problems later in life. These problems are typically the result of life experiences stored in emotionally dysfunctional ways in the brain and not sufficiently processed. When the emotions from these early experiences are stirred up by current situations, the brain cannot synchronize or regulate emotion appropriately, and dysfunctional behavior results. If the dysfunction and lack of synchronization is severe, neuroses and psychoses result; if the level is significantly less severe, the result is one or more of the retroactions we have discussed—confusion, perfectionism, defensiveness, resistance, or discouragement—and a loss of energy and focus.

A dramatic example of how this kind of irrational fear robs us of confidence is the story of Myron, a Director of Marketing for a medical devices company. Though he was one of the "golden boys" of the organization—young, bright, aggressive, and a tremendous leader—he had one fatal flaw that was mostly hidden. That flaw was an irrational fear of getting caught unprepared to speak in front of others. The fear was connected to the severe stutter he suffered with throughout his early school years.

For any event where he might possibly be called to speak, Myron would engage in hours of detailed preparation, complete with research, overhead transparencies of data analyses, and mental practice of how he would make his comments. This compulsive behavior served him well in most situations. Unfortunately, there were always those unplanned events like being called to speak to an unanticipated issue during a conference call, or being asked a few moments in advance to respond to a question raised at a large conference or network meeting.

When Myron's irrational fear kicked in, he would first become aware of tightness in his chest and shortness of breath. These were symptoms he could control without most people noticing. But as his fear heightened, his face and ears would begin to flush uncontrollably and his thoughts would get confused. Then he would become deathly afraid that someone would pose a question for which he was not thoroughly prepared, and he would stumble confusedly in his response. On the occasions when this did happen, it caused him immense embarrassment in front of his colleagues. Myron's underlying irrational fear was centered on personal rejection from others.

When he became anxious in this way, Myron would use a number of coping strategies to hide his inner turmoil. Sometimes, he would take on a defensive edge to throw people off balance and shift the focus of discussion. Other times, he would pull way back into his mental shell or physically leave the room in order to avoid the spotlight. Both of these should be familiar from our discussion of the five retroactions in the last chapter. Each strategy he employed was designed to protect Myron from embarrassment and ultimately from rejection by others. However, these coping behaviors themselves were increasingly causing others to hold him at arm's length and to question his "golden boy" status.

Myron's strategies to protect himself from his irrational fear of personal rejection clearly got in the way of his unconditional acceptance by others, so why did he persist in using them? The answer is that he had developed a set of retroactions in this area. At one point in his childhood, Myron "discovered" that if he was totally prepared for every situation where he might need to speak in front of others, then his stuttering was held to a minimum and he felt "safe" from rejection. He began to believe something like this in his little boy brain: "If I am thoroughly prepared, then I won't stutter and people will not reject me." The fear of rejection, then, was bonded to the perfectionistic faulty belief that he must always be prepared for any situation.

It's easy enough to see how the stuttering led to a faulty belief about total preparation, but where did the fear of rejection originate? Because he was emotionally sensitive and his parents were especially stern and critical, Myron began to be afraid that his parents did not really love him. His fear of rejection/abandonment developed from this. The stuttering complicated the situation and introduced a great deal of embarrassment to him and his parents. At some point in these early childhood years, he decided that if he did things right and was always perfectly prepared, his parents would show him love and acceptance. Though he was not consciously aware of the reason for the fear or his faulty beliefs, they continued to dramatically impact his adult life. We will learn more about Myron as we formally introduce the concept of faulty beliefs in the next chapter.

REFLECTION MOMENT—QUESTIONS TO CONSIDER

Take some time now to thoughtfully consider your answers to these questions, and capture them here or write them on a separate sheet of paper. You can use your responses to focus your thinking and to share with others in a discussion group based on this book.

1. **Which fundamental irrational fear—personal rejection, role insignificance, or irreparable hurt—is the one that you believe gets stirred up in you to kick off a thoughtless reaction?**

2. **In what ways did your parents show you that they loved you (typical ways include telling you in spoken or written words, doing nice things for you, buying you gifts, spending time with you, putting their focus primarily on you, touching you supportively)? To what extent did you actually feel loved by them? How do you wish they would have showed their love for you?**

3. **What painful or fearful memories do you recall from the earliest part of your childhood, before age seven? In what ways might the fears from these events continue to have a negative effect on you as an adult?**

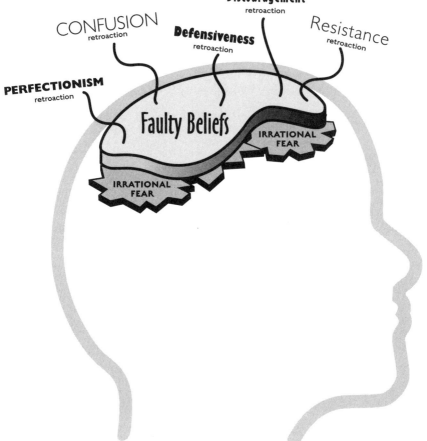

4

Driven by Faulty Beliefs

As we have seen with our discussion of Myron in the last chapter, the underlying irrational fear of rejection tended to become agitated in situations where his stuttering could possibly occur. When this fear was worked up a bit, a belief would click in that "If I am thoroughly prepared, then I won't stutter and people will not reject me." Myron could see as an adult that this conclusion about being perfectly prepared was not a rational one; it was impossible in most cases and it would not guarantee a successful outcome every time. However, that did not stop this faulty belief from bonding with his fear of rejection to create defensive and avoiding behaviors when he found himself in situations for which he was not totally prepared.

Together, these components in Myron—the fear of rejection and the faulty belief in total preparation—formed a compound that rivaled a diamond in hardness and persistence. While it is possible that some level of preparation did, in fact, keep him from stuttering in some situations, and that speaking without stuttering protected him from rejection a time or two, it is also possible that preparation had nothing whatever to do with his stuttering or acceptance by others. It is even possible that his anxiety about being totally prepared actually made his stutter worse.

Whether or not it was a valid strategy, the fact is that Myron believed it would help, and then he compulsively engaged in this preparation behavior before each known event. That is, he took a strategy that seemed rational and effective and utilized it in such a perfectionistic way that it became an irrational strategy. After a number of years, it also became unconscious as the original fear and faulty thinking got covered with layers of life experiences. His current behavior in stressful situations was then driven by unconscious, irrational fears and faulty beliefs.

WHAT ARE FAULTY BELIEFS? They can most easily be thought of as "if, then" statements that start with the belief and end with the false promise of protection. As in the case of Myron, he thought to himself, "If I am thoroughly prepared, then I won't stutter and people will not reject me." Myron and I came to this understanding of what one of his faulty beliefs must be through a deductive process. That is, he did not literally remember having thought this as a small child 40 years earlier, but together he and I looked at the kinds of retroactions that he tended to exhibit since childhood. We identified one behavior as a compulsive need to be perfectly prepared for any task he faced that required him to interact with others whose respect and acceptance he desired.

In identifying this typical behavior that he and others might observe, we actually discovered a "vapor trail" that led us to the faulty belief underneath. If perfectionistic, compulsive preparation was the behavior on the outside, we reasoned, there must be a faulty belief on the inside that directs him to behave in this way. Like solving for an unknown variable in an algebraic equation (math phobics stick with me for a moment!), we deduced his underlying belief. Setting this situation into basic algebra, we came up with this formula that follows the simple algebraic $F + X = B$ equation, where F is irrational fear and B is observable behavior:

Fear of Rejection + X = Perfectionistic Preparation for Events

Myron had previously identified his F variable to be fear of rejection, and we knew that when this fear and some unknown faulty belief (X) combined inside the limbic system of his brain, the resulting behavior (B) usually looked like the retroaction of perfectionistic preparation. Consequently, we used our logic to deduce that the missing piece of information, X, must be a faulty belief that went something like, "If I am thoroughly prepared, then I won't stutter and people will not reject me."

In my own life in the last 10 years, I have become increasingly better at recognizing the vapor trail of fears and faulty beliefs that undermine my high performance behaviors. One of my most persistent combinations is the following:

Fear of Rejection + Belief About Pulling Back = Shy Behavior

Shy behavior in one sense comes fairly naturally to me, since I am an introvert and my father was an introvert. However, when I get shy in situations that require the opposite behavior, it becomes a problem. In a recent situation, I was invited to a session at a large, multinational client of mine who had just developed its own 360-degree, multi-rater feedback form and wanted all of its preferred vendor executive coaches to become familiar with the instrument. I arrived a few minutes early and paused at the door to look around the room for people I might know. Of the dozen or so people at the session, I recognized only one other executive coach and the woman, Mindy, who coordinated coaching assignments as part of her human resources role.

In that moment as I hesitated and scoped out the room, another woman came up to me and extended her hand. She said her name was Linda, and she briefly introduced herself as someone who worked with Mindy. I smiled and greeted her, and then looked back at the room to decide my next course of action in this group of people I did not know. I was feeling shy and not very interested in making small talk, and Linda stood next to me in silence for a moment or two before she moved into the room. I followed her lead.

It was not until several weeks later that I found out that Linda, who I had assumed played a secondary role, was actually the person who was chosen to replace Mindy in her coaching coordinator role. Linda, then, was the person I needed to get to know so that she was comfortable referring coaching clients to me. I arranged to meet with her to more completely introduce myself and learn about her and how she viewed her new role. In the course of our talking, I started to describe the concepts in this book and how I used the perspective in my coaching. I even used myself as an example, as I have throughout this book, and explained how fear of rejection often led to shy behavior on my part. As I spoke, a smile began to spread slowly across her face.

"I noticed that behavior when we first met," she said, "and I interpreted it as lack of confidence. In fact, I have a potential coaching client for you who is a very strong, assertive female, and I'm not sure you would be confident and strong enough to handle her." In that moment, I realized that she was giving me some painful and revealing real-time feedback that helped me see how my "shy" behavior on the inside could easily be interpreted as lacking confidence by an outside observer. We had a very open conversation after that, and she decided to connect me to this woman as her coach. The woman's story, in fact, is one of those you will encounter later in this book.

From Myron's story and my brief anecdote about Linda, it is clear how the combination of underlying fear and faulty belief generates retroactions that are not very effective. While there are many different variations and subtle nuances in the faulty beliefs that you and others hold to be true, there are some patterns that can be teased out to help you recognize your own set of beliefs. The data summarized, below, come from 40 people whose demographics represent two thirds males and one third females, with ages ranging from early 30s to mid-fifties. Each of them is a professional, manager, or executive working in for-profit and non-profit organizations ranging across multiple industries.

The key in identifying your faulty beliefs is to look at the behavior that is observable by you and others, and then to determine what the underlying thinking must be. To help you in this quest, here are the top seven faulty beliefs I have encountered in my coaching work:

> **If** I get shy around people, check out or leave, hold back my affection, put up a wall, hunker down, keep people at a distance, avoid interactions, wait until it blows over, or become who they want me to be, **then** I will not say or do something wrong to be rejected by them.

> **If** I hesitate, put things off, pull back from a decision, carefully analyze to make sure it's the right decision, or thoroughly think things through, **then** I will protect myself from looking incompetent.

> **If** I undersell myself, don't push others or upset them, don't make waves, or if I make a joke about it to diffuse the tension, **then** I won't get hurt.

> **If** I prove or explain myself, handle everything and get credit for it, deliver the results, fix the problem, do exactly what people want me to do, fulfill my part perfectly, say yes to their requests, show them they can rely on me, work really hard and stay constantly busy, or the best, **then** I will be seen by others as worthy.

> **If** I show people that I know everything, am clever/ smart, never make mistakes, always make the right decision, always have the right answer to a question or problem, am totally prepared, can figure it out on my own, under-promise and over-deliver, **then** they will like me.

If I am in control, show no faults, always contribute ideas, don't waste time, achieve success, have a large impact, put things into the order they should be in, don't let others take control or mess it up somehow, **then** I will look good and people will accept me.

If I aggressively get into people's faces, act sarcastically, attack them to get their attention, express who I am, convince them, pound my point home, or force them to see I am right, **then** they will include me, value me.

The actual number of possible faulty beliefs is very great and we will illustrate more of them as various other people are introduced in the book. For now, it is important to understand that these kinds of beliefs are faulty for two major reasons. First, they have their origin in early childhood, well before you were capable of logical analysis. Since they began before logic, they are pre-logical or irrational in nature. The promise held within such beliefs is always naïve, childlike, and simplistic. Second, they have become unconscious over the years so that we are not aware in our rational minds that we are thinking these thoughts. Nonetheless, they give direction to our behavior. Being influenced as an adult by a set of beliefs that are both irrational and unconscious can create a dangerous situation.

Of course, while all beliefs developed before logic begins at about age seven are "pre-logical," and therefore irrational, they are not always faulty. For example, if a young boy believes that his parents love him, that it is good to share toys, or that hitting his sister is usually a bad idea, these are not "faulty" beliefs even though they have their origin in early childhood. We are concerned here with those beliefs that are based on irrational thinking that follow closely on the heels of an upsetting event and that hold a false promise of protection for the child. These beliefs are faulty in the sense that they almost never actually provide protection—as a child or as an adult.

Even in the most idyllic, happy childhood characterized by highly functional and effective parenting, events occur that can cause distress and lead to the pairing of irrational fears and faulty beliefs. What seems innocuous and innocent on the outside can feel scary on the inside and create some powerful fears and faulty beliefs. For example, my young daughter, Kate, and I were riding bikes one day and we had our Golden Retriever named Max with us. As we made our way down the road, I suddenly became aware of a car rapidly approaching us. At the same moment, I realized that Max and I were on one side of the road, and Kate was on the other. I called to her to quickly join us, but then realized there was not enough time to pull the three of us together. I quickly yelled to Kate to stay put on her side of the road.

With two opposite commands, she got a scared, confused look on her face and stood motionless until just before the car came around the corner, and then she started to come toward me. I screamed helplessly for her to stop, the driver slammed on the brakes, and the car's tires screeched to a halt just before the front bumper hit Kate. I started to yell some more out of fear and agitation, and Kate began to cry. It was a moment of great upset, and the fear of getting hurt in a way she could not fix took root in Kate's pre-logical mind.

CHILDHOOD FEARS. As we have briefly discussed, faulty beliefs develop in the same way that our underlying, irrational fears are born—in a moment of upset from early childhood. Sometime during the years from two to seven, most children experience a strong fearful emotion. Events that elicit such fears could be something fairly simple, such as being in the grocery store with your mom and losing track of her while you were looking at the toy you could get inside a box of cereal. Though she may have been only an aisle away from you, the fear that you had been left behind or that she disappeared forever might have caused instant panic in you. Or, you may have been one of those children who experienced persistent or traumatic physical, emotional, or other abuse at the hands of your parents, trusted adults, or older siblings.

Whatever your personal history might include, some type of fearful event or series of events happens to each one of us in these early childhood years, and when it occurs, an irrational fear develops around whether or not we are loved, respected, or safe. Right on the heels of that fear, a faulty belief germinates about how we must protect ourselves in the future from such an upsetting event. As with my daughter, even a happy, supportive childhood and upbringing can be marred by an upsetting event or two that plants irrational fears and illogical beliefs. In coaching individuals with happy, idyllic childhoods, it is often more difficult to identify the origins of their fears and faulty beliefs because nothing stands out as having been a problem or issue. As we dig together in conversation about the early years, however, we usually find an event or two that, while not terribly dramatic, could have resulted in their irrational fears and beliefs.

LANGUAGE AND LOGIC. It is during this period of early childhood from age two to age seven that language develops to the point that we can generate full sentences and complete thoughts, but our logical analysis has not yet begun to function. Typically, logic does not begin to show until after age seven, and is not fully formed until age 12 or the early teen years. Any belief we create during this early childhood period must be illogical at the core, since it develops before our brains are capable of logical perspective. As noted, the promise held within your faulty beliefs is naïve and simplistic, and often not true. We develop faulty beliefs to protect ourselves from harm, but usually end up getting in the way of our own effectiveness.

As a quick reminder, this is how the connection to the past happens in the present:

- A current event occurs.
- Association is made in our subconscious mind with an upsetting memory event from childhood.
- Untrue statements (anchor lies) about ourselves from the memory event stir up irrational fears inside us (personal rejection, role insignificance, or irreparable hurt).
- The irrational fears connect with one or more faulty beliefs.
- These fears and faulty beliefs are immediately transferred to the present situation.
- We react thoughtlessly, and others around us see our retroactions.

In adulthood, most of the time as we behave in response to our faulty beliefs, we create the exact opposite of the intended effect—just as Myron did in the previous chapter in situations where he was not totally prepared and was afraid he would stutter. But something also happened at a deeper, more vulnerable level within Myron. In addition to the faulty beliefs that drove him to always be perfectly prepared in every situation he faced, he began to formulate and hold onto a belief about himself—about who he was and why people would never fully accept him throughout his life. It was a fundamental lie that he began to believe—one that held his fear and faulty beliefs in place and convinced him that he was "not worthy of being loved by others." We turn in the next chapter to an in-depth discussion of these fundamental or "anchor" lies.

REFLECTION MOMENT—QUESTIONS TO CONSIDER

Take some time now to thoughtfully consider your answers to these questions, and capture them here or write them on a separate sheet of paper. You can use your responses to focus your thinking and to share with others in a discussion group based on this book.

1. Which one or more of the top seven faulty beliefs seem closest to what you tend to be thinking when you engage in your retroactions?

2. There are probably people from your work or home life who are in a position to see your retroactions and give you helpful feedback on what they look like. Ask them for feedback and capture their thoughts, here, on how they perceive your behavior when you get stressed:

3. Fill in the following equation with your most typical irrational fear, faulty belief, and retroaction:

> **Fear of** _____
>
> **+ Belief that I** _____
>
> **= Retroaction of** _____

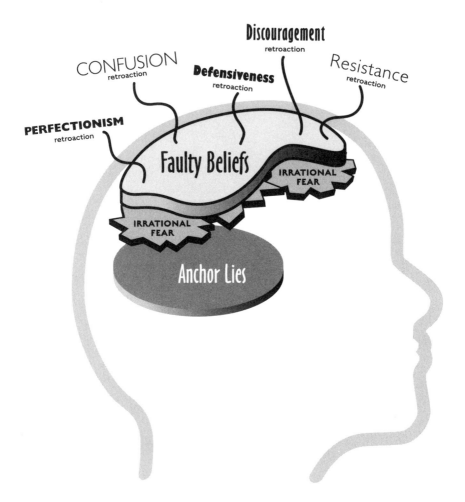

5

The Lies that Blind

Several years ago, a coaching client raised an important question by sharing an early irrational fear experience from her life. Sally started by saying, "You know, I'm confused about this retroaction thing and why the underlying fears and faulty beliefs continue to have an effect on my life today. For example, I have had irrational fears in the past that no longer plague me, so why would my fear of failure still be hanging around when these others have disappeared?"

"That's a great question," I responded. "Give me an example of an earlier fear that no longer affects you."

"Well, okay, here is the best example I can think of right now. When I was about five years old, my parents bought me a new, shiny red bicycle for my birthday. It had a fancy seat on it and reflectors in the spokes and it had a wonderful, new smell. It had two extra wheels in the back that kept it upright, so I took it out to the driveway right away and rode around in circles with a big smile on my face and my hair blowing in the wind. I loved it so much I wanted to sleep with it that night! This love affair with my new bicycle went on for several months, until I discovered my parents' devious little plot.

"They used this 4-wheeled bike to wean me off my trusty tricycle, and then announced one day that it was 'time to take off the training wheels.' 'No!' I shouted, and I began to cry—'don't do anything to change my perfect bike! Don't make me ride without the special wheels—I'll fall down and hurt myself really badly like Joey did down the block'."

"So, you were pretty frightened about the prospect of trying to balance on just half of those wheels?" I asked.

"Yes," she responded, "and I was certain that I would crash into the curb or a prickly bush or a tree and get really hurt and be laughed at by my older brother. In spite of protests from me, my dad took off the little wheels and then sat me up on the seat of this two-wheeled death-trap. He steadied it with one hand behind the seat and the other on the handle bars, and then took off running down the driveway with me and the bike between his outstretched arms.

"By this time, I was so frightened, I became hysterical. I was crying and yelling at him to stop, but he just kept pushing me in a big circle in the driveway. Eventually, we both started to tire and I stopped crying when I realized that I hadn't fallen so far. With my feet still going around in a circle on the pedals and my hands gripping tightly to the red handle-grips, I started to think that maybe I could actually do this two-wheeler thing. In a short while—I have no sense of how much time it actually took—my dad had me out on the sidewalk, balancing and going straight. I kept pedaling and before I even realized it, my dad was no longer holding on to the bike and I was excitedly wheeling past the neighbors' houses.

"So, the fear was gone then?" I interjected.

"It was gone. I even learned to stop and get on and off by myself that day. I also fell once or twice, and discovered that it really didn't hurt that much and I was able to get right back on that red bike in a wink. Here's the thing, though. I haven't ridden a bike in several years, but I know that if I took my 12-speed down from the garage rafters and dusted it off, I would not be afraid to ride it. Tell me why that irrational fear of falling on the two-wheeler would just disappear over time after I realized that it was not a real fear, but my fear of messing up at work on a visible project has not gone away even though I now know that it's irrational?"

Sally's question was a great one, and it came at a time when my reading and insight from coaching clients began to suggest an answer that was quite simple: the bicycle fear was not anchored in Sally's brain to any persistent belief about herself. It is possible the bicycle fear was connected to an irrational fear of rejection, insignificance, or getting hurt and it might have been supported by a faulty belief. However, the bicycle fear was not central to Sally's beliefs about herself and her acceptability to others, and it dissipated once the new bicycle skill was mastered.

By way of contrast, her fear of failing at a major project at work was held fast by something negative Sally believed about herself; consequently, she continued to experience irrational fear and to react with perfectionism even though I had been trying to "steady her two-wheeler." I had helped her see that this fear of failure at work was just her retroaction in operation, and reminded her that she had had a number of successful project "rides" to provide her with evidence to the contrary. Still, she persisted in worrying about her ability to be successful and to avoid failure at work. It became clear to me that she held on to a lie deep inside the recesses of her brain, and this lie provided an immovable anchor for the fears and faulty beliefs she experienced at work.

Serving as a foundation for the retroactions that you and I experience, such a lie originates in early childhood. We will refer to these as **anchor lies.** Whereas faulty beliefs are irrational, false "if, then" statements that tell us what we need to do to protect ourselves, anchor lies tell us why we are fundamentally unacceptable to others. If we each believed at the deepest level that we were fully acceptable just as we are, then there would exist no lasting foothold for the irrational fears and faulty beliefs that might develop in our childhood. However, in observing ourselves and others around us, just the opposite seems to be true.

The notion that there exists in us an underlying, anchor lie helps explain the habitual pattern of retroactions in which people engage throughout their lives. In the last chapter, we met Myron and were introduced to the concept that his compulsion to always be totally prepared was under-girded by an anchor lie, "I am not worthy of being loved." It is sad for me personally to learn about adults like Myron who grow up with this kind of fear-based lie. Yet I know from my coaching experience with others and insight about my own childhood that every child grows up with a lie that undermines his or her self-concept and self-confidence. I also see the evidence of such lies in my own two children and realize that in spite of our best efforts as parents, these lies slip in and take root. Most often, parents are the direct or indirect cause of these anchor lies and are totally oblivious to how they became lodged inside their children's emotional memories.

It makes me even sadder when I talk to people like Dan, whose fear of irreparable hurt developed because of the way he was treated by his father. He described for me the time, at six years old, when he accidentally spilled some vegetables at the dinner table while trying to put them on his plate by himself. Instead of encouraging his son's initiative and independence, his father got angry about the small mess on the tabletop. To punish him, his father sternly forced Dan to put his plate on the floor next to the dog's dish and finish eating his dinner down there. Crying and ashamed, Dan sat on the floor away from the rest of the family and ate with the dog. This sent a clear message—though I assume one unintended by his father—that Dan was on his own and that no one, including his father and his mother, would be there to protect him when he was sad or hurt. He began to believe the anchor lie that he was all alone in life, and he often behaved in a cold, distant way that unintentionally ensured that this lie would feel true.

Let's look more closely at these irrational, unconscious lies that provide the anchor for our retroactions. Think back to your own life during this period from age two to age seven. Perhaps you have limited or no memories from this part of your life, or perhaps pictures, sounds, and smells easily come flooding back. Try to imagine a situation in which you were afraid or embarrassed or feeling very alone. The memory you recall may seem rather trivial and unimportant, or it may be quite traumatic and upsetting as you re-live it in your mind. Whatever you remember, it may hold a key to naming the anchor lie you believe and cling to.

No matter how emotionally and financially healthy the family was in which you grew up, or how idyllic your childhood, you experienced an event or series of events in which you felt some strong negative emotions. When the event occurred, you responded the best way you knew how as a young child. A mental picture of the event and the feelings associated with it became stored in your memory. Over the years, the event and feelings have become imbedded so deeply in your mind that you may not be consciously aware of them anymore.

So, why is this important to figure out at this stage in your life? Why not just let the past stay in the past, the old painful wounds remain bandaged up in some dusty closet of your mind? For this reason: a current life situation will often stir up the same emotional pain you felt as a child, and you will begin to react in the irrational ways we have been discussing. Here, again, is how the connection to the past happens:

- A current event occurs.

- Association is made in our subconscious mind
  with an upsetting memory event from childhood,
  ages two through seven.

- Untrue statements (anchor lies) about ourselves from the memory event stir up irrational fears inside us (personal rejection, role insignificance, or irreparable hurt).

- The irrational fears connect with one or more faulty beliefs.

- These fears and faulty beliefs are immediately transferred to the present situation.

- We react thoughtlessly, and others around us see our retroactions (confusion, perfectionism, defensiveness, resistance, or discouragement).

You might wonder, "How many lies actually exist inside me?" My coaching experience suggests that, while there could be an infinite number of variations of such lies, they can be distilled down to five most typical **anchor lies.** Usually, only one or perhaps two of them are ones that you hold at a deep level to be true of yourself:

> **Abandonment**—"I will never experience love, nobody cares about me or accepts me; I am alone, not lovable."
>
> **Shamefulness**—"I am nobody, and I need to hide who I am; I can never be forgiven; I will always be tainted, will never amount to anything; I don't deserve the acceptance of others."
>
> **Invalidation**—"I'm too weak or stupid to do anything right; I cannot do anything on my own; I am not worthy or important, not respected in any way."

Hopelessness—"I will never be happy or whole in my life; nothing good will ever happen for me, and I cannot trust anyone to help me."

Alienation—"I'm different from the others, standing alone; I'm weird, odd, or strange in their eyes; no one understands me or wants to get to know me."

These five lies represent a distillation of numerous possible variations on the counterfeit theme, and they have one general thrust in common. Each one of them represents a belief aimed at your core self and each supports the underlying conclusion, *"there's something wrong with me."* It's almost as if each one of us as a child experienced an important adult screaming at us out of frustration and anger, "What's wrong with you?!" and we each silently responded with one or more of the anchor lies, above. How is it that some early events result in lies and faulty beliefs, while others do not? That answer is not known for certain, but we can speculate that it is related to the degree of internal upset the event causes. Events that from the outside seem quite traumatic may leave minimal wounds, while events that seem quite innocuous from an observer's point of view may create massive emotional wounds on the inside.

A few typical patterns are presented on the next page to illustrate the way the anchor lies and irrational fears may have gotten started and supported inside you. Clearly, there are many possible patterns; these are intended to get you thinking about what yours might be, not to provide an exhaustive list.

The underlying retroactions and anchor lies can be thought of as connected to each other at a deep level in our brains, as we have discussed in chapter 3. When the irrational fear on the left becomes activated by a current event and a faulty belief kicks in, the resulting retroaction will only be noticeably strong if the anchor lie is also hooked. There are likely many times during a typical day, for example, when you react a little defensively, feel a bit discouraged, or become slightly confused. If this results in only a minor reaction on your part, your anchor lie probably was not involved.

Early Event	Irrational Fear	Anchor Lie	Faulty Belief	Retroaction
Criticized for being too spontaneous	Personal Rejection	I'm different, no one understands me: Alienation	"Avoiding others keeps me from being criticized"	Resistance (passive/avoiding)
Seen by others in the family as "different"	Personal Rejection	I don't deserve love: Shamefulness	"Must hide from others, not take a strong stand"	Confusion
Treated with hostility, contempt by early teacher	Role Insignificance	I'm not respected or worthy: Invalidation	"Even if I try my best, it won't be good enough"	Discouragement
Having fun, but suddenly upset or hurt by a parent	Irreparable Hurt	No one is here to protect me: Abandonment	"I will be safe if I'm always ready to protect myself"	Defensiveness
Laughed at by older sibling for not knowing something	Role Insignificance	Can't trust anyone to help me: Hopelessness	"I need to always have the right answers, figure it out myself"	Perfectionism (Controlling)

Another way to think of your retroactions and the faulty beliefs that contribute to them is that these are the visible evidence of you engaging in coping behaviors that are for the most part ineffective. Your faulty beliefs reflect your attempt as a little child to come up with a strategy to protect yourself from being traumatized now and in the future. These kinds of strategies are nearly always ineffective in helping you cope overall, but they might appear to help you in the short term. For example, passively avoiding someone because your feelings are very hurt and you want to make sure you don't cry in front of him or her is a coping strategy that might appear to be helpful right now. However, the long-term implications of avoiding contact with someone who has hurt your feelings may not be very helpful at all, particularly in a marriage or deep friendship.

As we discussed earlier, these retroactions originate in childhood, roughly from age two to age seven. For each of us as children, something occurs that at the time is frightening and threatens our needs for acceptance, significance, and safety. This event or series of events, our feelings about the situation, and the beliefs we formed right then to guide our future actions all become stored in the non-logical, non-conscious part of our brains. The chart on the previous page creates a framework which pulls these components together with some coherence, but what does this phenomenon look like in real life?

The people used here to illustrate how retroactions develop and impact behavior are from the same 40 recent coaching clients referred to in an earlier chapter. Two thirds of them are males and one third females, with ages ranging from early 30s to mid-fifties. Each is a professional, manager, or executive working in for-profit and non-profit organizations ranging across multiple industries. Though this sample is not large enough to conduct formal research, it provides a depth of anecdotal data to clearly depict how effectiveness is undermined by these factors. Of the 40 clients, 45 percent were deemed to be dealing with the anchor lie of invalidation, followed by 20 percent with the lie of abandonment, 15 percent dealing with the lie of shamefulness, and 10 percent each with the lie of alienation or hopelessness.

Let us start with an example of how the most prevalent lie—invalidation—begins and lives in a couple of my coaching clients. It should be noted again that, though these stories are based on actual cases, the names have been changed and in most cases the gender, type of organization, or functional area of the individual have also been altered.

> **"I'm too weak or stupid to do anything right;**
> **I cannot do anything on my own; I am not**
> **worthy or important, not respected in any way."**

INVALIDATION—SANDRA'S STORY. Born and raised on the family farm with an older brother and younger sister, Sandra grew up with a dad who she described as distant and unemotional but fairly well educated. Her mom was the pillar of the family, a disciplinarian who raised the kids, but would have preferred to be working outside the home. Dad wanted his wife to stay home with the kids and she acquiesced to that wish, but never really seemed happy with the decision. Sandra perceived her dad to be the weaker of her two parents, with Mom much more dominant in decisions the family made. Sandra spent some special times with her dad, and consequently felt somewhat closer to him than to her mother.

Though she could not remember a specific incident that might have triggered her underlying irrational fears or the anchor lie, Sandra indicated that she grew up not liking to be told what to do and getting into some trouble for that. Her older brother seemed to be more adept at working the farm; consequently, Sandra was beset by **irrational fears** related to her own competence and significance in the family. She identified the **anchor lie** "I am not worthy" (invalidation) as the one that undermines her confidence even now.

In her current role, Sandra works as Director of Quality Assurance for a mid-sized manufacturing company. When I began coaching with her, she was being considered for a promotion to the top role in her area, but some people making that decision were concerned about her abrasive effect on the people on her team and her peers. On a 360-degree feedback instrument given inside the organization (filled out by her, her manager, direct reports, and peers to rate her leadership strengths and weaknesses), she was described by others as aggressive and dominant, inclined to jump in and take over if she perceived that things were not going well, somewhat out of balance in the time she spent at work, and not a very effective listener or collaborator.

As Sandra and I talked early on in the coaching, she began to express some of her frustrations with her work situation and the people on her team. It became clear that when her irrational fear of role insignificance became stirred up due to the situation around her, the lie "I am not worthy" kicked in and she unconsciously began to react. In her case, her **retroactions** were a combination of resistance and perfectionism. When the fears became aroused by the situation, she started taking over, pushing people around and trying to rigidly control the process to make sure it did not become derailed. Some of the **faulty beliefs** we identified that gave direction to her behavior included the following:

> "If I say I'm going to get a project done, I have to at all costs; I must always without fail deliver no matter what the circumstances."

> "If I'm not getting the job done, I must put in more hours because I'm not that smart—I just work harder than the others do."

> "If I just keep talking here, the right two bullet points will come to me and I will use them to convince people I am right."

> "If others don't include me in the decision, then they're discounting me."

Reading through these faulty beliefs, you can see the themes of talking fast, trying to convince others, pushing to get results regardless of the effect on others, and reacting negatively when she perceives that she is not included in the decision-making. Sandra also noticed that just before these irrational fears and faulty beliefs clicked, she usually began to react viscerally—typically by talking faster and beginning to perspire. At the same time, her thoughts became less clear and it seemed even harder for her to make the kind of points that would convince others she was correct in her thought process. The ironic thing is that she usually was right in her thinking in the first place, but worked way too hard to convince others, and not hard enough to listen to their perspective and include them in the final decision.

INVALIDATION—JOHN'S STORY. The fifth of seven children, John grew up in a traditional family where Dad worked and Mom stayed home with the kids. The parents gave plenty of hugs and kisses and words of love to him and his siblings and acted like best friends as a couple. However, when Dad would drink and stay out until late at night, his parents would fight and Mom would talk divorce. John's friends loved his dad because of his personality, and he would talk proudly of his son, but not usually directly to him. John was a hard worker in school and at home, and he was employed at jobs outside the home when he got old enough. This hard work ethic seemed to be expected by both parents, but some of John's siblings were not required to work and were given more opportunities than John had. He began to think that maybe he was not worthy of anything special and his lot in life was to just work hard and get things done.

As his career began to develop after college, John got involved in the field of Human Resources and eventually worked his way up to Director of Human Resources for a major architectural firm. In this role, others saw John as someone who encouraged a fun and energized environment, who was collaborative and open with them, who was direct and exhibited integrity in his interactions with them, and who set high standards and worked determinedly toward objectives. Their comments and scores on a multi-rater feedback instrument also depicted him as someone who could be a bit too controlling at times, who had difficulty delegating and letting go of things, and who seemed to get a bit agitated and defensive when things got stressful.

Generally confident and take-charge in most situations in his role, John became noticeably less comfortable and clear when he was in a situation where he was unable to articulate an idea or perspective. He became agitated when people did not understand how big a particular problem was, or the potential impact when people were being treated badly in the organization. When he became frustrated in this type of situation, his face felt hot and started to turn red, and he began to talk somewhat sarcastically to those who did not "get it." Then he started to feel confused about what to do next and became defensive if people questioned his stance on the issue.

John was a bit surprised by the feedback he received on his multi-rater instrument, but not so much by the critical comments and ratings. Mostly, he was surprised that others rated him so highly, and he seemed a bit embarrassed that their comments were so positive and glowing. The paradox with John was that, even though his underlying **irrational fear** was that people would not see him as competent and would not like him, he didn't want to come across as too highly functioning because others might feel bad when they compared themselves to him. He had created for himself a sort of psychological box in which he was driven to be highly effective, but did not want others to feel bad if they were less effective. When the **anchor lie** of invalidation—"I'm not good enough; I don't warrant any positive attention"—got engaged and his underlying fear of looking insignificant clicked in, he began to operate based on some of the following **faulty beliefs:**

> "I must make sure I have all the facts and have not missed a step, or I will feel stupid."

> "I must minimize what I do so I don't get the attention on me, because I wouldn't have anything smart or interesting to offer."

> "If something goes wrong, I must take responsibility for it so that no one else feels bad."

> "I never want to imposition people or inconvenience them, or it will embarrass me or look like I don't try hard enough."

When his fears and faulty beliefs became enmeshed with each other and his anchor lie of invalidation was hooked, John's **retroaction** behavior looked confused and defensive. When he acted confused, others would step in and try to direct him; this reaction on their part only served to make him feel less competent and more confused. If he became defensive to their feedback and comments, they tended to become argumentative and defensive themselves. As was the case with Sandra, the harder John tried to look competent without making others feel bad about their level of competence, the more confusing it became for everyone. The paradox is that the more people like Sandra and John work to come across as competent, the less confidence people around them actually have in them, because they seem to be trying too hard. We look next at the anchor lie of abandonment.

"I will never experience love, nobody cares about me or accepts me; I am alone, not lovable."

ABANDONMENT—PETER'S STORY. The youngest of eight children, Peter's mother was emotionally stressed much of the time as he grew up and frequently "checked out." The kids often had to fend for themselves, with little help from their father. When she got upset, his mom would yell and scream, dump stuff on the floor, and threaten things like, "I'm going to leave—I can't put up with this!" Consequently, Peter was constantly afraid that he would do something to upset her and make her leave. His dad was the postmaster of a small town, and before that had run a little barber shop on Main Street. When his mother was not upset, she could be quite expressive in her love for Peter, showing interest in his activities and nurturing him with hugs.

When he went off to school, Peter started out well in kindergarten, but felt a bit different from the other kids because he was having trouble seeing the blackboard. Later that year, he started to wear glasses to correct his eyesight, and the kids teased him about being a "four-eyes." The following year, in first grade, he experienced difficulty learning to read. He got quite emotionally distraught when reading time came around, and this began to affect his school experience in general. To help him improve, his parents and older siblings read to him and listened to him read, but it was not enough to save him from having to repeat first grade the next year. In later elementary years and throughout his schooling, Peter reported that he grew up "fiercely independent."

Flash forward to Peter in his current role as Brand Manager for a medium-sized manufacturer of personal care products. When we first met to discuss the possibility of engaging in a coaching relationship, he indicated that he wanted to work on building skills that would help him get to the next level in his company, as well as to become more effective at influencing others at a broader and deeper level in the organization. He had recently moved from a creative marketing role to the brand management role, in which he had an increase in direct reports and leadership responsibilities.

One of the areas which he mentioned in our second meeting that was somewhat troublesome for him was his lack of confidence at this new level of leadership. The personality testing and multi-rater feedback we gathered showed him to be someone who was assertive, results-driven, independent, creative, humble, energetic, and empathetic. The results also reflected a man who tended to procrastinate and who was somewhat perfectionistic. He was seen as someone who wanted to be in control of things, but was so open to others' opinions that he often did not hold confidently to his own perspective when a firm decision was needed.

As we talked together during the first several sessions, it became clear that Peter was more likely to lack confidence in a few specific situations at work. For example, he tended to feel uncertain that he would be seen positively or that he would be effective in getting his message across when he met or presented to senior managers in a large group. He worried about performing poorly in front of them or failing them somehow, and not being able to influence their perspective.

When his **underlying fear** of personal rejection first became stirred up in these situations, he usually felt a general sense of anxiety. His **anchor lie** of abandonment would then get hooked and he would begin to feel less confident in his ability to function effectively. This was often followed quickly by the appearance of one or more of his **retroactions**—feeling confused, not confident, and wanting to resist the control of others through avoidance of the interaction altogether. When these retroactions appeared, his behavior was directed by such **faulty beliefs** as:

> "I shouldn't bother these people; I'll just quietly do my job and let them do theirs."

> "If I ask my boss about this to get his perspective, it will only bug him—I need to figure it out on my own."

> "I don't want to be dependent on these people— I can't trust them and I can take care of it on my own."

These faulty beliefs reflect the pattern of his retroaction behavior—avoiding situations, not wanting others to exert control over him, not trusting their intentions or capacities, and not wanting to appear incapable in their eyes because they might not like him. Others noticed Peter's behavior on several levels and their comments and ratings on his multi-rater feedback report reflected lower scores on creating teams with multiple perspectives, soliciting and analyzing various ideas before making decisions, and seeking the perspective of others. Clearly, when his faulty beliefs clicked in, he came across as closed to others' perspectives—the opposite of the effect he was trying to create.

ABANDONMENT—JEANNE'S STORY. Since her father was in sales and was very success-oriented, every time he got promoted the family had to uproot and move to another part of the country. Mom stayed home while Dad traveled a lot for his work, so he was not around for many of Jeanne's school events or things like piano and dance recitals. When he was at home, Jeanne's dad was not very expressive of his love for her or for her two siblings. Jeanne remembers being somewhat anxious and uneasy as a child and she went through a period of time when she had lots of nightmares. In particular, she remembers having a nightmare one night when she was about four years old and climbing into bed with her parents for comfort. Instead, they rebuffed her and told her to go back to her own bed. Jeanne had to attend lots of new schools and try to make friends with many new kids as she grew up. She reported that she became shy around people she did not know, and she remembered feeling physically ill when the family moved during her late elementary school years.

In her current role as Director of Merchandising for a retail apparel company, Jeanne often finds herself working with product developers, designers, and vendors whom she does not know well. In these situations, she has learned to develop a level of confidence and comfort, but once in a while she will start feeling shy and anxious. These fearful feelings usually come up when she is around lots of people she does not know, or when someone reacts to her thoughts and perspective in a way that makes her feel incompetent or wrong. What she notices first in these situations is that her thoughts begin to race, and then she feels the blood pressure building inside her chest. At this point, she usually starts to react in a short-tempered, defensive manner as she tries to wrestle control of the situation away from others so that they won't mess it up somehow. Her **retroactions** of defensiveness and perfectionism become readily apparent for those with a discerning eye.

As we began to work together, Jeanne realized that in situations like the ones described, the scared little girl inside of her tries desperately to take control of the situation and protect her from her **irrational fears** of appearing incompetent and not being loved by others. Her **anchor lie** of abandonment—not being worthy of love—starts to stir and she becomes reactive rather than responsive in a mature, adult way. In moments like these, as she regresses to become more like one of her children than her adult self, she begins to recognize that these **faulty beliefs** drive her behavior:

> "If someone disagrees or wants to challenge my approach, they're telling me I'm incompetent."
>
> "If I don't do my end of the project perfectly, then I can't be assertive with someone else about their part of it."
>
> "No matter how well I do something, I can't feel good about it because I could have done it better."
>
> "People won't automatically care about who I am or what I have to say, so I must convince them about my perspective."
>
> "If I have ownership of it, I need to drive it to a successful conclusion, no matter who gets in the way."

Jeanne's story, like Peter's, illustrates how the anchor lie of abandonment can originate and how it can cripple someone's day-to-day effectiveness. Next, we will discuss the anchor lie of shamefulness.

> **"I am nobody, and I need to hide who I am; I can never be forgiven; I will always be tainted, will never amount to anything; I don't deserve the acceptance of others."**

SHAMEFULNESS—INGRID'S STORY. The youngest of two children with almost a dozen years between her brother and her, Ingrid's childhood memories are mostly about people checking out on her or leaving. Her older brother was never in the same school as she was, so he never wanted to play with her as she was growing up. He left home when she was still in elementary school. When he was living in the house, she often felt left behind by him as he headed out the door without her to go to school or to work. Dad was a sales manager who drank liberally and became more demanding when he did so—especially when dealing with her mother. Ingrid's mother was fairly unassertive and seemed to just meekly accept his disrespectful and hurtful comments. Though her father often joked that Ingrid was "adopted," she was clearly Daddy's little girl and the apple of his eye.

In spite of his attention, Ingrid grew up feeling unloved by her family. Her parents never said they loved her, but instead gave her cards and stuffed animals. She felt that they must not really love her because they would not say it directly, and at some point her **irrational fear** of personal rejection developed. As a result of this upbringing, Ingrid does not have much patience for women who seem weak or passive—like her mother—and she tends to "act out" as a test of whether or not others will really love her and stick with her. She is driven to be in control and to be involved and included in activities at her work, where she functions as the VP of Engineering for a growing computer storage device company. In her work, she tends to react in a "mean, self-centered" way when male authority figures around her appear to be rejecting her.

With all the irrational fear of rejection in her background and continuing to the present, one might think that Ingrid's anchor lie would be focused on abandonment issues such as not being loved or accepted. However, in her little-girl mind during the ages of two to seven, she came up with a different slant, which she describes in her adult voice as, "I must not be a good person, because if I were, people wouldn't want to leave me." Every time her brother or a parent checked out or left her, she interpreted it as meaning that she was not a good person, and that she was too mean or self-centered to be acceptable. Therefore, her primary **anchor lie** actually centers on shamefulness—not deserving the love or acceptance of others because of something missing in her. She also has the influence of abandonment as a secondary anchor lie.

When her fear of rejection becomes aroused in current situations, it hooks the lie that she is not deserving of acceptance and she begins to act out against that. First, she feels a "flipping" sensation in her gut, and then she begins to get agitated or angry. On the outside, she appears to suddenly get paralyzed (the confusion **retroaction**), and then evidences stubbornness and impatience (defensiveness, resistance, and perfectionism). Providing direction to her behavior, she begins to react based on **faulty beliefs** such as:

> "I need to be careful about how much I invest in any relationship, since they might abandon me in the end."

> "I have to be aggressive enough to make sure I'm included, valued."

> "You're either with me or against me, and I need to test which it is."

> "I need to abandon him/her first, before he/she abandons me."

> "I must protect myself from other people taking me down by the choices they make."

SHAMEFULNESS—KEVIN'S STORY. Kevin grew up in a mid-sized town as the youngest of three. His older siblings were both girls and were much older than he. All of them had grown up taking on chores and responsibilities related to his father's small retail business, but the burden fell stronger on Kevin because he was the only male and because his father had developed heart disease a year or two after his son was born. As a result of his dad's physical limitations, Kevin often stepped in as the male and became quite adept at doing the work that needed to get done at the store.

Because of his father's limited energy each day, most of the time Kevin spent with him was focused on getting a chore done and he didn't get the kind of fatherly advice regarding things like sports that other boys his age got . In fact, Kevin remembers playing baseball on the school playground in the third grade and having his friends yell at him to "choke up on the bat," but he didn't have a clue what that meant. It was embarrassing to him that his dad was not as able-bodied as his friends' fathers seemed to be, and that he did not get the kind of fatherly perspective and focus other guys seemed to get. His **irrational fear** of personal rejection developed from these situations.

Kevin grew up in a strict religious home where he learned about what was right and what was wrong, but did not learn much about grace or compassion. Because he had engaged in some behaviors in his childhood and adolescence that he knew his parents would consider shameful and wrong, he began to believe that he could never be truly forgiven in God's eyes. In current work situations, when Kevin begins to wonder whether or not he has the right facts someone else requested of him, he starts to feel tense and begins to sweat. Acting confused at times and defensive at other times, he procrastinates out of the need to make sure he is able to do things perfectly. These **retroactions** become more and more evident to others as they become frustrated with his behaviors. From early childhood, he began to believe the **anchor lie** of shamefulness—that he could never be forgiven. By the time he grew to an adult, a series of **faulty beliefs** that focused mostly on doing or saying things right so that he would not become embarrassed were fully formed in his brain:

"If I'm wrong, or if I lose the argument, then people won't value me."

"If things change quickly and I don't have time to process and get prepared or talk it through thoroughly, people will view me negatively."

"If people don't inform me of things that are happening, I must not be important enough to be included, so I just need to pull back, batten down the hatches, and be safe."

This focus on being right so he would not be embarrassed or ashamed rarely protected him from the negative reactions of others. In fact, it usually made Kevin react in defensive and perfectionist ways that turned other people off and made them more likely to conclude that he was being embarrassingly stupid. Like Ingrid, his faulty beliefs drove a type of behavior that got in the way and made him appear less approachable and less competent. Consequently, it was difficult for people to get close to him. Often, people like Ingrid and Kevin who have perfectionistic tendencies become somewhat discouraged over time because of their perceived inability to impact others.

We look next at the anchor lie of hopelessness. It is important to distinguish between a person stuck in the lie of hopelessness, and an individual suffering from diagnosed clinical depression. While for example, the negativity caused by years of unfulfilled hope in a person's life can be discouraging, it does not necessarily reflect clinical depression nor an anchor lie related to hopelessness. Only a licensed mental health professional such as a psychologist specializing in depressive disorders can make an accurate diagnosis. Hopelessness as described here is intended to create a greater understanding for those who are not currently or likely to be diagnosed as clinically depressed, but who often feel overwhelmed or pessimistic.

> **"I will never be happy or whole in my life; nothing good will ever happen for me, and I cannot trust anyone to help me."**

HOPELESSNESS—ERNIE'S STORY. The youngest of three children, Ernie had two older sisters who were three and five years his senior and who were very good students in school. Ernie, on the other hand, struggled a bit with learning and was especially weak in mathematics. He reported being more or less on his own because both his father and mother worked and his sisters were not very interested in helping him succeed in school. His mother was a school nurse and his father worked as a personnel manager after having left the teaching profession. Dad was not very demonstrative with his love—only occasionally meting out praise and never giving any hugs—while Mom was a hugger and more accepting of Ernie's behavior. In thinking about his relationship with his father, Ernie said that he never felt as though he could do anything in school that would be good enough to get his dad's approval, since he was not athletic or artistic or good in math. Later in high school, Ernie began to excel in Speech Communications and for the first time felt good about himself as a learner. He was also very involved in scouting and eventually earned his Eagle Scout award.

In Ernie's case, it seems clear that the lack of any significantly close relationship with his father is the base of his fears and faulty beliefs. The controller for a large consumer electronics company, Ernie indicated that when he finds himself in work situations where he is not totally prepared for someone's question, he immediately starts to lose confidence in himself and feel anxious, and then becomes passive and confused. In further discussion with me, he began to understand that these "early warning" reactions provide a clear sign that his underlying **irrational fears** of insignificance—not looking competent—have just became aroused. He identified his **anchor lie** as that of hopelessness and recognized that when this lie becomes hooked, he thinks to himself, "Nothing I do will ever be good enough." The situations that act as a catalyst for his irrational reactions are often those in which it seems to Ernie that someone is trying to take away his control, when he is uncertain of an answer, or when others seem to be challenging him in a disrespectful or condescending manner.

When one of these types of situations occurs, he quickly engages in **retroactions** ranging from defensiveness—arguing, becoming stubborn, talking down to people—to perfectionism, in which he becomes rigidly controlling or procrastinating. Often, he finds himself holding people at arm's length, putting up high walls built on distrust, and failing to develop relationships with them. Together, we identified these **faulty beliefs** that drive his retroactions:

> "If someone asks a question, I must know the answer and respond correctly, otherwise I will not look capable; any question of me by another is

designed to challenge my knowledge and ability, so I must fight it somehow."

"I can't be wrong or I will look incompetent, but I can't rely on others to have the right answer, either. If I screw up, I'm going to get yelled at, so I can't make a mistake."

"I must always be in control, in charge, and presenting myself as confident and valuable."

"I just need to hunker down and avoid people until things settle down."

With these kinds of faulty beliefs, it is not surprising that Ernie's managers and co-workers often see him vacillate between being an arrogant, condescending know-it-all, and a confused, uncertain conflict avoider. When I first met him, his behavior had already resulted in his being fired from senior positions in two different companies. These unexpected and painful occurrences led him to desire to understand why he was shooting himself in the foot, and to develop some new strategies and interpersonal tools to make sure his lies and faulty beliefs never again were allowed to get in the way of his success.

HOPELESSNESS—GARTH'S STORY. The second oldest of five children and the oldest son, Garth was rather rebellious as a child—pushing the boundaries at home and at school and behaving in ways that had an irritating effect on his relationship with his mom. His father, who owned and operated a service station in town, never had much time for Garth when he was a small child. In the late elementary grades, Garth started working at the service station. His father was fairly controlling, however, and did not seem to trust Garth to do any of the skilled tasks at the station; he also seemed unwilling to actually teach his son how to do the tasks correctly.

Though he was quite successful in school, Garth began to doubt his own competence and adequacy. Because of his early experiences with his father, he developed the **irrational fear** of appearing incompetent and inadequate. He was easily frustrated and often worried about the best way to respond to problems that arose. Later in his career as an actuary for a financial services firm, he made life difficult for people around him. Exhibiting his **retroaction** of resistance, he rebelled against rules and those in authority over him—often treating them disdainfully—and did not trust that they had his best interests in mind. Usually refusing help from others because he was not sure of their true intentions, Garth exhibited a pessimistic attitude about projects and people.

On some level, he believed the **anchor lie** that no matter what he did, nothing good was ever going to happen for him, and that the best he could hope for was to resist the control of others and defend himself when attacked. He tended to debate with others in a defensive, hard-nosed style that was ineffective in getting his objectives accomplished. Others viewed him as a person who did not team up well with peers but who was tenaciously protective of his direct reports. When he was not trying to drive his point home, Garth often disappeared and avoided situations due to his doubts about being able to create any kind of change.

These behaviors were not always present, but were more likely to come out when he felt like others were taking a shot at his team, reacting to something about the actuarial group without having credible facts, or deceitfully playing the game outside the rules. The **faulty beliefs** that guided his behaviors at these times included these:

> "If I don't attack these people and out-debate them, I will look bad."

> "They are just looking for someone to pick on, trying to make an issue out of nothing, and I must show others that they are wrong."

> "If someone is being purposely hurtful to a person on my team, I have to deal with in a way that ensures that I will not lose."

Ernie and Garth illustrate a kind of desperation that develops out of the anchor lie of hopelessness. Often, there is an overwhelming need to prove that you are right and competent, and at the same time a strong undercurrent of discouragement at ever convincing others of your point of view. When Ernie or Garth felt hopeless, they either lashed out in a desperate attempt to prove their worth or pulled way back and avoided the confrontation altogether.

Our last anchor lie to discuss is that of alienation.

"I'm different from the others, standing alone; I'm weird, odd, or strange in their eyes; no one understands me or wants to get to know me."

ALIENATION—MATT'S STORY. Matt's father was a successful sales manager who was frequently promoted to organizations located in other parts of the country. Consequently, Matt and his family tended to move quite often as his father found new positions. As you might expect from a sales manager, his dad was outgoing and quite comfortable socially; however, his mother and Matt were much more reserved. An only child, Matt did not feel much emotional support when he headed out to the school bus to start classes at another new school. Because his personality type is fairly introverted, Matt tended to make friends superficially at school. He purposely avoided developing long-lasting, deep friendships because he knew that he would be moving again the next year or the following one.

Underneath, Matt began to develop an **irrational fear** of appearing incompetent due to the difficulty he experienced feeling comfortable building relationships at home and at school. As he stood alone on another first day at another new school, he started to think of himself as being very different from the others, and concluded that no one would want to know him or to really understand him. He began to believe the **anchor lie** of alienation.

In his role as an academic dean for a large university, Matt often found himself in meetings with other senior leaders where he would disengage and not participate in the discussion. When he surveyed the room, he saw people who seemed different than he on so many levels—people who were brighter, more intellectual, more politically savvy, or more capable of influencing the decisions of the rest. In unstructured social situations, he tended to pull inside himself, get shy, and pick out one or two people to focus on and connect with while he ignored the larger group.

His stomach tightened and he felt anxious and overwhelmed in these situations; it became difficult to prioritize his thinking. Then, some combination of these **faulty beliefs** would begin to give direction to his subsequent behavior:

> "If I make a mistake, it's going to look bad and people won't have confidence in me."

> "If I don't know anything about a subject or I'm not interested in it, people won't accept me."

> "I'm not very good at being socially engaging, and I would be uncomfortable trying."

> "I will only be acceptable if I use a 'sneak attack' mode, where I try to influence people behind the scenes in subtle ways that don't call attention to me."

From his multi-rater feedback, it is clear that others see him as having high integrity, excellent insight when he shares it, and good skills at creating effective teams. They also indicated that he has a great sense of humor—when he exhibits it—and a strongly organized and planful approach to his work. However, they wanted him to be more vocal in sharing his opinion in meetings, to be more actively collaborative by seeking other perspectives, and to show more passion and energy in presenting his point of view. Their comments also suggested that he play more of a devil's advocate in his role, that he function with a greater sense of urgency, and that he be less defensive about his own mistakes and those of his department. From their feedback, it is clear how Matt's feelings of being different lead to **retroaction** behaviors that are, at their worst, defensive, avoiding, and not confident.

ALIENATION—ED'S STORY. The family environment where Ed grew up was described by him as a chaotic one in which eight kids—including his three brothers and four sisters—mostly just ran around. When Ed was five years old, his younger sister was born and he remembers feeling ignored by his mother. Before his sister came along, Ed remembers tagging along with his dad when he worked at night as an electrician. He also fondly remembers Dad letting him drive the truck one day on the way to a favorite fishing hole. In some ways, these warm memories of time with his dad made the situation when he was six years old even more painful. That was the year that his father was killed in an automobile accident, and a friend of the family sat all of the kids down to give them the horrible news. Ed remembers that his sisters burst into tears and that he wanted very badly to do the same, but his three older brothers just sat there in stoic silence. He chose to mimic his brothers, thinking that was what a man should do, and stuffed his grief inside.

After that incident, Ed's mom spent even less time with him and more time with the two youngest kids. She took his siblings and him to school, tucked them in at night, and occasionally ruffled their hair or hugged them, but there was precious little time for each child. Ed was left to work things out in his own head and heart, and he began to feel the **irrational fear** that he just didn't measure up in the minds of his brothers, his friends, and adults around him. He felt different from others—he was the one without a dad, he was the one who wanted to cry when his brothers responded like true men. It became hard for him to trust others and let them get close, because he felt so alienated from them. He began to believe the **anchor lie** that he was a stranger who must stand alone. It felt as though he had no one to open up to, to be close to, or to tell about his hurt. Consequently, he retreated deep inside himself and tried to work things out in his mind.

As he got older and began his career, he quickly became involved in the field of computers, where he could focus on projects and not worry about trusting others. He became knowledgeable in software applications and worked as a consultant for several larger firms until one day he decided to go out on his own. Initially, he worked as a software consultant, but eventually he developed enough business to start his own small company. When I met him, he was the president of this small organization and was having some difficulty creating a team of senior managers below him. It was difficult for him to think in terms of teams, and he tended to exhibit the **retroaction** of perfectionism by holding others at arm's length and communicating only minimally with them while he tried to control things.

It was clear after talking with Ed a bit that his anchor lie of alienation was keeping him separate from others on his team and causing a great deal of distrust. Particularly in situations where he couldn't figure out where people were coming from or where there was an awkward silence and he didn't feel as though he was connecting with them, he started to disengage and think that he was the odd one in the group. At these times, he felt discouraged and one or more of these **faulty beliefs** directed his reaction:

"I'm the odd one in this group; I don't want to talk about this, don't want to become a social outcast."

"If I take some sort of action here and it lets others down, I wouldn't know what to do."

"If I share personal things with people, it sets me up for rejection; if they don't know me, they can't hurt me."

"If I'm not in control and don't know where an interaction is going, then I might not know what my reaction is supposed to be."

For Matt and Ed, the anchor lie of alienation and the fear that somehow they would not be acceptable to others if they knew who they really were, got in the way of their developing intimate, trusting relationships. Instead, they came across as guarded and closed in many situations, or presented an outward persona that was not truly who they were. Keep in mind that anchor lies provide the foundation for fears and faulty beliefs and they are deeply rooted in the non-rational, limbic part of the brain.

You now have the full model of what stops you and others from leading fearlessly in your work and lives. When a situation on the outside hooks your anchor lie, it also usually stirs up irrational fears and faulty beliefs that drive your retroaction into a typical pattern.

OBSERVATION ABOUT ANCHOR LIES. In talking with scores of individuals through my executive coaching, it is clear that most people can identify one primary lie that seems to be the anchor holding their fears and faulty beliefs in place. Sometimes, people identify a couple of anchor lies that appear to be at the bottom of their retroactions. These people can usually identify one as the primary anchor lie and the other one as a secondary lie. On rare occasion, individuals cannot distinguish one anchor lie from another in their own life. It is possible, then, that people might manifest more than one distinct anchor lie at times, or a hybrid of more than one anchor lie. The most typical pattern, however, is that one of the five anchor lies is more central than the others.

Now that you have a fairly good idea about what might be derailing you in your life, the question becomes "What can you do about it?" Part of the answer lies in getting progressively better at recognizing these retroactions when you see them in yourself and knowing that they always come from the same source of fears, beliefs, and lies. In addition, it is critical to develop a strategy for changing your irrational reactions into high performance responses. That is the focus of our next chapter.

REFLECTION MOMENT—QUESTIONS TO CONSIDER

Take some time now to thoughtfully consider your answers to these questions, and capture them here or write them on a separate sheet of paper. You can use your responses to focus your thinking and to share with others in a discussion group based on this book.

I. Think again of an event from your early childhood where you felt afraid, embarrassed, or upset in some way. How might this event be related to the anchor lie that you have developed?

2. In looking at the five anchor lies and reading the stories that illustrate each, which one(s) of these lies (abandonment, shamefulness, invalidation, hopelessness, alienation) seem to you to hold fast your faulty beliefs and irrational fears (rejection, insignificance, or hurt)?

3. In what way do you see evidence for this anchor lie in your normal daily activities; that is, how does it get in the way for you?

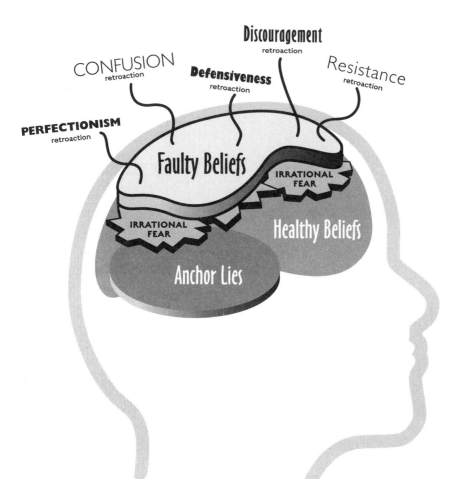

6

Steps to Fearless Breakthrough

The insights and perspectives discussed so far are critical to establishing an understanding of how anchor lies and fears get in the way of your optimal day-to-day effectiveness. This chapter will help you move past your retroactions and become free to live your life and fearlessly lead others based on healthy beliefs and high performance behaviors. The key is to fully understand the role of lies, irrational fears, and faulty beliefs in making you stumble, and then to catch yourself when you begin to react thoughtlessly to situations around you so that you can respond in a highly effective manner. This is the essence of a fearless breakthrough.

The following anecdote, shared with me in an email by a coaching client named Joe, will help illustrate the point. After having been introduced to the retroactions in his own work and life, Joe, Marketing Manager for a large department store retailer, shared this story about how he was beginning to use the insights and perspective: "My team was meeting with the individual who was planning to conduct some focus groups for us, and one of the goals was to analyze the relationship between the stores, catalogs, and website. Our department has some very big goals this year, and I intended to use a good deal of what this meeting came up with to inform our decisions about redesigning the webpage.

"However, once the meeting got rolling, the direction of the focus groups shifted to more of a holistic view of our customer —not much emphasis at all on the website. I felt myself getting increasingly upset and feeling the need to convince everyone at the meeting that we needed actionable items regarding the website, but they all came down on the side of the broader approach. In reaction to this, I began to really push my point and become defensive about my position. My stomach tightened up.

"Recognizing that my fear of insignificance—not being seen as a contributor—had just gotten stirred up, I stepped back and asked myself, 'why am I so afraid of being wrong here?' It was obvious that they were all on the same page and I was the one who was out of step. I realized in that moment that I was terrified of failing the larger challenge of redesigning the website, and I was hoping that the focus groups would miraculously provide the perfect answer for me. I also recognized that it was threatening to me to have all these other people lined up on the opposite side of the argument because I respected their opinions so much. The whole situation made me very doubtful about whether I had anything to contribute to this group, since I seemed to be so wrong."

This simple story from Joe's workday illustrates a couple very profound and important perspectives on the effect of lies and faulty beliefs. First, these thoughtless behaviors occur in reaction to external situations—like people not seeming to listen or acting as though they disagree with our own thoughts. When our reactions occur, we are often aware on some level that they are inappropriate and ineffective. Joe's over-reaction was evident to himself and others as he raised his voice, became tense and agitated, and aggressively pushed in support of his opinion. Second, others start to react in their own way to what they perceive as an over-reaction on our part. In Joe's case, the group seemed to become even more galvanized in opposition to his point of view. This is typical of what happens when someone launches into a thoughtless reaction; people's backbones stiffen and it becomes even more difficult to get to the intended goal or to reach a decision. As he later noted to me, "I spent most of my time pushing a point that wasn't going to change. Besides killing momentum and wasting time, I felt like I needed to speak to everyone afterwards to make sure they knew I was now on board with the direction they had decided to take. It was NOT a great feeling!"

Perhaps most important, Joe's story illustrates an effective strategy for getting past such an irrational reaction. Though difficult to use consistently and quickly, the strategy he learned and later applied in this situation is quite simple. We call it the **Steps to Fearless Breakthrough:**

1. Identify catalyst situations—become aware of events that most typically stir up your lies (abandonment, shamefulness, invalidation, hopelessness, or alienation) and your retroactions (confusion, defensiveness, resistance, perfectionism, or discouragement). Usually, you will see a pattern from the past that can serve as a warning when a retroaction might occur again in the future.

2. Be on the alert within yourself for your "early warning" symptoms. The quicker you recognize a reaction in progress, the easier it is to circumvent. Your body usually gives you signals that the fears/lies have become agitated, often with symptoms like feeling anxious, tense, flushed, agitated, confused, or having tightness in neck, stomach, shoulders, etc.

3. Ask yourself this question: "What in this situation is causing me to feel my irrational fear (rejection, insignificance, hurt)? Or ask yourself, "What is hooking my anchor lie (abandonment, shamefulness, invalidation, hopelessness, or alienation)?" Asking either question introduces a rational, conscious question into an irrational, unconscious fear reaction. It is sometimes difficult to recognize who or what is causing the fear/lie to become stirred up. It helps to consider "Who's the **audience** here?" that is, who am I most afraid of disappointing, being unacceptable to, getting hurt by? Just by posing the question in your mind, the fear/lie usually lessens or disappears and your normal, high performance response mode takes over.

4. Get perspective on the situation by asking the follow-on question, "How big a deal is this?" or "What's the worst that could happen here?" or "Will this still be important five years from now?" This type of question helps lessen the effect of your faulty beliefs by giving you perspective on the situation you face. Most of the time, you are not dealing with life-or-death situations. Even when you are, having the proper rational perspective on them will be helpful.

5. Reinforce your healthy beliefs by reminding yourself what you as a rational adult truly believe in these situations. Speak your new, healthy beliefs to yourself to counterbalance the compounded impact of reacting out of your faulty beliefs for so many years of your life up to this point.

6. Establish the bedrock truth about yourself by recognizing when your early childhood lie gets hooked, determining what the actual truth is about you, and continuously reminding yourself of it.

7. Act on the truth of your new beliefs by getting more and more effective at the first six steps in this process and by continuing to develop yourself as a fearless leader.

The first thing that happened in Joe's story is that he recognized that he was working too hard to try to convince others of his opinion. Though he did not yet realize why he was reacting in this way, he did notice that he was upset and this helped him catch his defensive retroaction before it became fully blown. He was unaware of it at the time, but after further discussion he realized that often such situations in the past had resulted in defensive reactions on his part. That is, when others disagreed with him, ignored his perspective, or questioned his opinion, he more often tended to react with defensiveness or perfectionism. Joe realized that he could use this knowledge to help him anticipate his own level of reactivity and catch himself earlier on before his retroaction becomes fully blown.

At the moment of noticing his own reaction to the group, Joe asked himself why he was so afraid of being wrong. This was the perfect question for him to ask at this point, because his underlying, irrational fear had become aroused and he had begun to react out of his faulty beliefs. Some typical faulty beliefs he utilized in his work and life were these:

> "I must always be able to handle things and contribute, or they won't value me."

> "I need to always be right, to convince them so that they are in synch with me."

> "I must always get the credit I am due, or they won't value me."

In Joe's situation, when he asked himself what was making him feel afraid of being wrong, he clearly saw the problem even though he was actively upset. It doesn't always work this way; sometimes, you continue to feel upset even after you recognize where the reaction is coming from. In those cases, it is helpful to get perspective by asking yourself how important this situation actually is. The questions we suggest here—how big a deal is this, what's the worst that could happen, or will this still be important five years from now—are those that have seemed to work best for others in trying to get perspective on a situation.

What we *believe* in a particular situation is the determining factor for how we will behave in that situation. As we have discussed earlier in this book, our beliefs are anchored to a lie about who we are and are fed by irrational fears about what we must do to protect ourselves. Joe's **anchor lie** was that of alienation— "I am all alone, totally separate from others"—and he frequently found himself in situations like the one described here where he felt different from the others in a group. His underlying **irrational fear** was role insignificance—not feeling like he was important or a contributor. The situation described above clearly depicts his upset reaction when it appeared that his ideas and contributions were not valued by the others. The **audience** that he was most afraid of disappointing was his peers, because he truly wanted their respect and affirmation.

The problem, of course, was that his faulty beliefs often acted as a perceptual screen so that the only evidence he took into his mind supported his fear of being unimportant and his lie of being different from others in a negative way. Each time he started thinking, "I must always be able to handle things and contribute, or they won't value me," his reaction took shape and the **retroactions** of defensiveness and perfectionism became obvious to others in the group. In further discussion, he realized that his typical **catalyst situations** (ones that usually stirred up his lies and faulty beliefs) occurred when he met with the senior leadership team and felt that his ideas were totally ignored or dismissed, as well as other times when he felt unprepared or overwhelmed by his workload. For Joe, the **early warning** that these fears and faulty beliefs had just become aroused was an unsettled feeling in his stomach.

Once Joe comprehended these basic building blocks for his retroactions, we began to work on a deeper level of understanding. In discussing his childhood, he related that his parents divorced when he was about six years old and he lived with his mother and younger sister. From the early elementary years through high school, he moved often with his small family and ultimately attended 10 different schools. Joe was always "the new kid" in the classroom of others who had already established relationships and made best-friend connections. He always felt out of place.

Joe described the early days at each new school without a close friend, particularly at lunch when he sat alone or next to people with whom he did not feel relaxed. On the school bus, no one invited him to sit down; on the playground, no classmate called out to Joe to join in a game. Eventually, he made friends at each new school, but meanwhile, the lie that he was different and the fear that he would never be valued by others continued to grow and strengthen in his mind. He reported feeling in those days that there was no one to focus primarily on him, no one to make him feel special or loved.

From our discussion, Joe recognized that in the work meetings where he felt unimportant and under-valued, the little boy inside him was simply reliving these old moments on the playground, the bus, the classroom, and at home. As we noted earlier in the book, these moments are stored in the emotional memory part of the brain where they wait for a current situation to stir them up and impact present behavior. We started to work on recognizing his faulty beliefs at the moment they begin to affect his behavior, and then reinforcing **healthy beliefs** that reflect how he views things as a rational adult. For example, Joe identified one of his faulty beliefs as, "I'm not a good decision-maker." When I asked him what that meant, he indicated that he did not seem to make good decisions, or he was too slow in coming around to a conclusion.

Through our ensuing conversation, Joe refined this further to state, "I take too long to make decisions, or I don't make them at all." Thinking about his difficulty making decisions in this way, rather than "I'm not a good decision maker" gave us a direction to work toward in our quest to make him a better decision maker. I then asked him why he delayed or avoided decisions, and he said, "Because I'm too worried about making wrong decisions." This last response gave us a much clearer picture of the faulty belief problem we needed to solve.

Depicting himself as "not a good decision-maker" had left us both somewhat de-energized about ever changing the situation, but revising the description to "I take too long to make decisions" gave us an opportunity to focus on his perfectionism. The issue was not that Joe was a bad decision-maker, but that his fears and faulty beliefs caused him to worry about and procrastinate so long on the decisions he needed to make that sometimes he did not make them at all! We decided that a healthy belief about making decisions would be: "Any decision I make is something I can learn from, and I can change it if it turns out badly."

Joe and I developed a grid of faulty beliefs and their corresponding healthy beliefs that looked like this:

Faulty Beliefs:

"I'm not a good decision maker, so I must avoid them in order to be viewed as competent."

"I must always be able to handle things, be an idea contributor, or they won't give me credit."

"I need to always have all the facts, do all the due diligence, and be right about things or I will fail."

Healthy Beliefs:

"Any decision I make is something I can learn from, and change if it turns out badly."

"I am valued most when I achieve results through others."

"It's not just me that the success of this project hinges on, so I need to involve others in it."

Joe immediately understood the model and began to apply these seven steps in his life. However, it became clear in the first several weeks that a large part of his approach to more effective behaviors involved recognizing catalyst situations and early warnings, and then stuffing his typical reaction to the situation in order to appear "more professional." I gently explained to him that the preferred approach was not to stuff feelings down deep inside himself and try to ignore them, nor was it to use affirmations to try to change his behaviors. Rather, it was to bring into his conscious mind the recognition of what was happening under the surface with his fears, faulty beliefs, and anchor lie. Then, his job was to reaffirm the truth of the situation in his own mind and guide his subsequent behavior through his newly identified healthy beliefs. I reminded Joe that getting better and better at catching the reaction cycle in the early stages would eventually reduce most of the power of these faulty beliefs in his work and life, and help him develop a long-term, healthy attitude.

It is an important distinction for the reader, as well. This approach is not built on stuffing feelings, stifling your reactions, or speaking affirmations in the hope of developing new behaviors. Instead, it is based on the powerful combination of recognizing when your unconscious, irrational lies and fears get aroused, and then choosing to respond with high performance behaviors based on your healthy beliefs. When you do this, you respond to situations in the most effective way possible. Initially, Joe understood the importance of the seven steps to fearless leadership, but did not completely engage in them or follow through with a fully fearless response. He created his own shortened version that featured the part about stuffing feelings and changing external behaviors.

Perhaps a second example would help you more fully understand how these components work together. Keep in mind that we are using this **Steps to Fearless Breakthrough** process for getting past retroactions:

1. Identify catalyst situations—become aware of events that most typically stir up your lies (abandonment, shamefulness, invalidation, hopelessness, or alienation) and your retroactions (confusion, defensiveness, resistance, perfectionism, or discouragement). Usually, you will see a pattern from the past that can serve as a warning when a retroaction might occur again in the future.

2. Be on the alert within yourself for your "early warning" symptoms. The quicker you recognize a reaction in progress, the easier it is to circumvent. Your body usually gives you signals that the fears/lies have become agitated, often with symptoms like feeling anxious, tense, flushed, agitated, confused, or having tightness in neck, stomach, shoulders, etc.

3. Ask yourself this question: "What in this situation is causing me to feel my irrational fear (rejection, insignificance, hurt)? Or ask yourself, "What is hooking my anchor lie (abandonment, shamefulness, invalidation, hopelessness, or alienation)?" Asking either question introduces a rational, conscious question into an irrational, unconscious fear reaction. It is sometimes difficult to recognize who or what is causing the fear/lie to become stirred up. It helps to consider "Who's the **audience** here?" that is, who am I most afraid of disappointing, being unacceptable to, getting hurt by? Just by posing the question in your mind, the fear/lie usually lessens or disappears and your normal, high performance response mode takes over.

4. Get perspective on the situation by asking the follow-on question, "How big a deal is this?" or "What's the worst that could happen here?" or "Will this still be important five years from now?" This type of question helps lessen the effect of your faulty beliefs by giving you perspective on the situation you face. Most of the time, you are not dealing with life-or-death situations. Even when you are, having the proper rational perspective on them will be helpful.

5. Reinforce your healthy beliefs by reminding yourself what you as a rational adult truly believe in these situations. Speak your new, healthy beliefs to yourself to counterbalance the compounded impact of reacting out of your faulty beliefs for so many years of your life up to this point.

6. Establish the bedrock truth about yourself by recognizing when your early childhood lie gets hooked, determining what the actual truth is about you, and continuously reminding yourself of it.

7. Act on the truth of your new beliefs by getting more and more effective at the first six steps in this process and by continuing to develop yourself as a fearless leader.

Mario grew up as the third of seven kids, the lower middle-class son of an Irish father and an Italian mother. His father was often stern, strict, and distant; he administered punishment with a belt or a paddle. His mother was somewhat aloof emotionally, but very encouraging to Mario and her other six children. In his eyes, she gave up her whole life to support the family. Mario's father was very adept with his hands and was always building or fixing things around the house, but Mario depicted himself as "totally incapable" of doing anything constructive manually. When he would help his father with projects, Mario often found himself the object of his father's rage because he would get confused about which tool he had been sent to retrieve. Neither parent expressed love with hugs, nor was Mario ever sure if his father really loved him.

Growing up a devout Catholic and attending parochial schools, Mario was very shy in the early grades, in part because he had a severe hearing problem brought on by abscesses in his ears. Quick to cry, he had trouble managing his emotions at home and at school. However, he was always a favorite of his teachers because he worked so diligently. The teachers did not recognize that his hard work was mostly driven by a tremendous fear of failure. Mario also became the star of the family through his academic efforts and, later on in high school, his prowess on the basketball court.

Both of these areas of success, unfortunately, were motivated by his deep, irrational fear of appearing incompetent. As he grew older and progressed in school, Mario turned his emotional sensitivity into repressed anger and found that he could express this on the basketball court in ways that actually contributed to his star status. Though he always was a top student in school, including college and graduate school, he described himself as "not very smart." He believed that he compensated for his lack of intellect by being articulate and aggressive.

As it was with Joe in our earlier story, Mario's underlying beliefs about himself determined how he behaved in life situations. In his case, his **faulty beliefs** were grounded in the **anchor lie** of shamefulness/invalidation—that he was not worthy and did not deserve the acceptance of others. For people like Mario who have many deep wounds from childhood, there exist multiple or compound lies and fears at the core. His reactions were particularly strong when the **audience** of his boss and others in authority over him seemed to view him as unacceptable in some way. He identified his underlying, **irrational fear** to be a combination of role insignificance and personal rejection. Often in situations of early childhood physical or psychological abuse like Mario's, it is difficult for people to distinguish which fear—personal rejection, role insignificance, or irreparable harm—is the predominant one that drives their behaviors.

His fears were most often agitated in situations where he was in a meeting of some sort and began to feel unimportant to the discussion. When this occurred, he typically felt restless and began to look around the room at others present in the discussion; anger welled up inside him. These were his **early warning** signals. As the anger quickly grew, he became sarcastic and arrogant, and then began to engage in a defiant assertion of his ideas or needs. His demeanor reflected his basic **retroactions** of resistance, defensiveness, and discouragement. When reacting in these situations, he took things personally, became controlling or adolescently defiant/argumentative, or was pessimistic and overwhelmed.

Together, Mario and I identified a number of faulty beliefs that typically arose to provide direction for his fearful reactions. Then, we began to generate a set of healthy beliefs that he could use to re-direct his behaviors. Here is the list we constructed:

Faulty Beliefs:	**Healthy Beliefs:**
"I must express who I am, regardless of the situation or nuance, and must make people accept me at all costs."	"When I fully express myself, others might not react positively to me, so before I speak, I need to ask myself if this will benefit others."
"I must prove that I am right, smart, quick-witted, strong at repartee, and willing to answer questions and take risks."	"I need to relax here and just be myself, without the arrogant defensiveness that puts people off."
"If I'm good, loyal, and honest all the time, people will understand and accept me in spite of my acting-out behaviors."	"Even if I don't knock myself out trying to be the good soldier, people will have a high respect for me as they get to know me."

As with Joe and Mario, the healthy beliefs here are intended to counteract faulty beliefs. They are designed to introduce a calm, logical, adult perspective that will eventually replace the edgy, irrational, childish beliefs directing our retroactions.

The purpose of this chapter was to help you re-examine the anchor lies and fears rooted in your past and to establish the conceptual groundwork for healthy beliefs and more consistently high performance behaviors in the future. As we discussed, your retroactions are anchored by a lie about you. In the following chapter, you will have an opportunity to more fully consider the healthy beliefs you would like to develop for yourself.

REFLECTION MOMENT—QUESTIONS TO CONSIDER

Take some time now to thoughtfully consider your answers
to these questions, and capture them here or write them on a
separate sheet of paper. You can use your responses to focus your
thinking and to share with others in a discussion group based on
this book.

**1. What are some situations during your typical day that
tend to set in motion your retroactions and anchor lies?
That is, what are your catalyst situations?**

**2. What is your "early warning" signal that your buttons just
got pushed? How do you tend to feel on the inside?**

**3. Who is the audience that you are most afraid of disap-
pointing, being unacceptable to, or getting hurt by?**

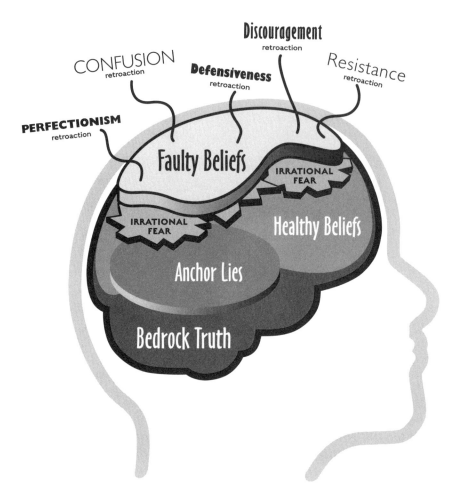

Nurturing Your Healthy Beliefs

As we established in earlier chapters, we each have a set of faulty beliefs that give direction to our behaviors as we react to a catalyst situation, and we can develop a counter-balancing set of healthy beliefs that help us respond more effectively and appropriately. The goal in developing healthy beliefs is to minimize the times when we react thoughtlessly in situations and maximize the times when we respond in a high performance manner. It is a major step to recognize what happens inside us as our anchor lies get hooked and we engage in our retroaction behaviors, but that insight alone will not generate new, more effective responses. These come about when we fully understand the extent of our faulty beliefs and replace them with a set of healthy beliefs based on adult logic and reason.

Though it is true that the faulty beliefs people hold inside their emotional memories are infinitely variable, the last chapter illustrated that these beliefs can be distilled into a finite number of prototypical ones. For each faulty belief, it is possible to identify a preferable healthy belief that is more effective to use in our daily lives. The following chart illustrates again the seven archetypal faulty beliefs we discussed in chapter 4, plus a healthy belief that could replace each one:

Faulty Beliefs:

"If I get shy around people, check out or leave, hold back my affection, put up a wall, hunker down, keep people at a distance, avoid interactions, wait until it blows over, or be who they want me to be, then I will not say or do something wrong to be rejected by them."

"If I hesitate, put things off, pull back from a decision, carefully analyze to make sure it's the right decision, or thoroughly think things through, then I will protect myself from looking incompetent."

"If I undersell myself, don't push others or upset them, don't make waves, or if I make a joke about it to diffuse the tension, then I won't get hurt."

"If I prove or explain myself, handle everything and get credit for it, deliver the results, fix the problem, do exactly what people want from me, fulfill my part perfectly, say yes to their requests, show them they can rely on me, work really hard and stay constantly busy, or the best, then I will be seen by others as worthy."

Healthy Beliefs:

"If I let people know who I am and I get to know them to a greater depth, then we are more likely to be able to work things out when problems arise."

"If I balance my need to think things through with the ability to make timely decisions, I will be most effective."

"Being calmly and consistently assertive with others is the most effective way to protect my interests."

"If I do my best to respond to the needs of others, and I let them know right away if I am unable to do what I agreed to, they will understand and respect me."

Faulty Beliefs, continued:

"If I show people that I know everything, am clever/smart, never make mistakes, always make the right decision, always have the right answer to a question or problem, am totally prepared, can figure it out on my own, under-promise and over-deliver, then they will like me."

"If I am in control, show no faults, always contribute ideas, don't waste time, achieve success, have a large impact, put things into the order they should be in, don't let others take control or mess it up somehow, then I will look good and people will accept me."

"If I aggressively get into people's faces, act sarcastically, attack them to get their attention, express who I am, convince them, pound my point home, or force them to see I am right, then they will include me, value me."

Healthy Beliefs, continued:

"I need to be responsive to people's questions and needs as they come up, but they don't expect me to have every fact at my fingertips. I can use others on my team to deliver on promises or keep track of important information."

"If I collaborate with others, solicit their ideas and feedback, and work with them to achieve success, they will value me."

"I will be the most valuable to others if I listen attentively to them, work cooperatively with them, and look for ways we can create win-win solutions."

This is not a complete description of all possible faulty/ healthy belief combinations. Rather, it represents a synthesis of those that have been shared with me and it covers the range of possible beliefs. You can use it to pick out the most typical faulty beliefs that get in your way, and then write down a healthy belief to counteract each faulty one on your list. Identifying new healthy beliefs will be a useless exercise if you have not done the preliminary work in the Reflection Moment sections of the chapters preceding this one. It's not too late to go back now and answer the questions there in order to build a foundation of understanding of the anchor lies, irrational fears, and faulty beliefs that have gotten in the way over your lifespan.

As you develop healthy beliefs to replace the faulty ones you have lived with all your life, they must be more than simple affirmations of who you want to become. They must be believable and sustainable, and they must reflect who you are at the very core of your personality. In general terms, your healthy beliefs should reflect how you think about yourself and your capacity to engage in highly effective behavior now that you understand your faulty beliefs. To put it into a computer analogy, the way you functioned when your irrational fears, faulty beliefs, and anchor lie were all operating is similar to how your computer functions when it is infected with a virus. If it functions at all, it does so in a slow, erratic manner.

Removing the virus on your computer is like replacing the faulty beliefs with healthy ones in your mind—suddenly you function at your peak effectiveness and you are all that you can be. However, removing the virus on a computer does not change its basic components; it still has the same central processing unit and software. In the same way, identifying faulty beliefs and developing healthy beliefs for yourself will only remove the impediments to your high performance behavior, not change the essence of who you are.

The goal of nurturing healthy beliefs is to get you back to the core of who you are and to help you be as effective as you can be with what you have. This necessitates knowing yourself now in a realistic way and recognizing who you are capable of becoming as your beliefs get healthier. Your new healthy beliefs must make sense to you and must be believable by you. As you work on them, it may seem to you that you are the character Bill Murray played in the movie, *Groundhog Day,* who kept trying over and over to get through the same day and get on to the next one. You must keep trying to catch yourself reacting to situations from your old irrational fears and anchor lie, and then shift your behavior based on your new, healthy beliefs.

Anchor lies and their attached fears and faulty beliefs attack the core of your identity and undermine your effectiveness. On some level, each faulty belief that you hold to be true hides who you really are. Continuing to function within your faulty beliefs is like eating junk food high in fat and refined sugars, whereas functioning with your new healthy beliefs is like eating a balanced meal rich in the proteins and complex carbohydrates your body and mind need to function optimally. Anchor lies and irrational fears can shut down your effectiveness in the same way that the usefulness of your computer is halted when the screen freezes. At the moment your computer locks up, you do not have access to any of the good stuff. Even though your hard drive, mother board, and software are intact, you are unable to access them until you re-boot the computer. Similarly, you have no access to the problem-solving capabilities, humor, or creativity of your cortex when irrational fear and lies become stirred up in the lower part of your brain.

Now that you have the motivation and means to begin to function based on a set of healthy beliefs, you are ready to explore the sixth step to fearless leadership—determining the bedrock truth. The next chapter explores several avenues for establishing the truth about you as a counterbalance to the anchor lie you have believed.

REFLECTION MOMENT—QUESTIONS TO CONSIDER

Take some time now to thoughtfully consider your answers to these questions, and capture them here or write them on a separate sheet of paper. You can use your responses to focus your thinking and to share with others in a discussion group based on this book.

I. If you could narrow down your faulty beliefs into two or three basic beliefs that get in your way at work and at home, what would these be?

2. Which healthy beliefs do you think it is important to nurture in yourself as a counter-balance to these faulty ones you have just listed?

3. Who are the people in your world, either at work or home, who "speak life" to you about who you are? That is, who do you know who encourages your healthy beliefs? How might you spend more time with them?

The Origin of Truth

In our seven-step process for becoming a fearless leader, we have discussed through step five—identifying healthy beliefs to replace your faulty ones. We have not yet addressed the concept of bedrock truth, which is the foundation for truly overcoming your lies, fears, and faulty beliefs. The **bedrock truth** is that deeply-held belief about who you are that exists at the very core of your being, and it tells you how acceptable you are to others in the world around you. It is bedrock because it provides the foundation for functioning in a healthy, effective way—not hindered by the anchor lie, faulty beliefs, or irrational fears. It is truth because it is based on how your worldview informs your thinking in the matter. In this chapter, we will discuss the topic from three very different worldview perspectives so that you can decide for yourself what is bedrock truth.

Most people are more comfortable with the concept of an anchor lie than with that of bedrock truth. Lies are entities for which we can see some evidence in our behavior and reactions to situations. It makes sense that something holds our lies and faulty beliefs in place and that this anchor is based on our foundational, negative thinking. The stretch is not too far to call this negative and inaccurate thinking about ourselves a "lie." The conscious, logical part of our minds can determine through objective analysis that we actually do not believe the lie that we are, for example, totally incompetent or not lovable. We can grapple with this intellectually because we see evidence for it in our day-to-day behaviors. However, understanding and accepting the idea that there is a bedrock truth about who we are that can be more powerful than the anchor lie requires us to go beyond logic and examine our deepest beliefs.

Each of us has grown up with one or more "world views" that informs the way we take in information and make sense of our perceptions. Some of us were raised with one world view and then exposed to a very different one when we went off to college or university, or when we moved from our birth country to a very different part of the world. In my lifetime, for example, I was raised in a home where we followed rules, believed in the benevolence of our elected officials, and went to church every Sunday. Then, I went off to college in 1968 and was exposed to a whole different style of thinking. I learned that rules and systems were made to be questioned and radically changed, that government officials were capable of lying and cheating, and that many people in the world believed in a different god than mine, in multiple gods, or in no god at all.

When I first became exposed to this kind of thought, I reacted to it by thinking that it was wrong-headed. Later on, as

I was more deeply immersed in it, I began to think of my early life ideas as wrong-headed. This was my first real experience with a clash between worldviews and my first taste of the truth from different perspectives.

Flash forward about 30 years to a professional conference I attended as a presenter and participant. The day started off with a keynote speaker whose topic was designed to help people slow down in their lives and attain a sense of peace and balance. Since I believe in the importance of these things in life and had spoken on the topic many times myself, I very much looked forward to his words. As he jumped enthusiastically into his topic, however, I began to get uncomfortable in the pit of my stomach. It took me awhile to recognize that my discomfort was connected to the philosophy that under-girded his presentation.

Without having identified his particular perspective to the audience, he was speaking the truth from his worldview, but addressing us as if it was the only truth. His assumption seemed to be that everyone in the audience believed in this same truth and that it was not necessary to label his philosophy. It was clear that he was blind to the fact that at least two other worldview philosophies were represented in the group that day. For the first time in 20 years of attending such conferences, I walked out of the large auditorium in silent protest of his failure to address this important disclosure. I also vowed to myself to identify my own worldview to audiences in the future so that people could know my philosophical underpinnings (see "About the Author" for this information).

So what are these worldviews I have introduced briefly? Well, the one I grew up with can be called the Monotheistic Faith worldview. This is clearly a religious worldview, based on the teachings of the Judeo-Christian and Islamic faiths, and it is part of the foundational fabric of North and South America, Europe, the Middle East, and various other countries around the world. When I went off to college at Northwestern University, I was quickly exposed to a second philosophy, which we will call the Naturalistic Humanism worldview. As we shall discover later in this chapter, this philosophical system is a religious-like one that believes in Nature rather than God, and that focuses on the role of self-actualization and the importance of social institutions in a person's development. The third perspective, illustrated briefly by my description of the conference I attended a few years ago comes from what we will call the New Age Mysticism worldview. In this philosophy, god exists in all things and there is a collective consciousness and a core belief that growth requires connecting to the god within ourselves. This view started in India and has spread in its various forms to the entire Far East and the West. I had also been exposed to this worldview while attending college.

This chapter is intended to provide you with a deeper understanding of these three competing worldviews, and to define the truth from each perspective. From historical records, the Monotheistic Faith worldview was the first to develop several thousand years ago, followed by New Age Mysticism (as evidenced in Buddhism, Hinduism, other Eastern religions, and Native American beliefs). The Naturalistic Humanism worldview is a relatively more recent development, with its earliest seeds planted by Greek and Roman philosophers and finally sprouting about a hundred years ago. In our discussion of these world-views, we will look at the source of the belief system, as well as the philosophy, psychology, and sociology of each. Then we will attempt to summarize the truth from each perspective. We will view them in approximate chronological order.

MONOTHEISTIC FAITH. The source of this worldview is contained in the Jewish Torah, the Islamic Koran, and the Christian Bible. The religions of Judaism, Islam, and Christianity believe in a single Supreme Being (called Jehovah by Jews, Allah by Muslims, and God by Christians) who is the creator and sustainer of all that exists. The sacred writings of the Koran were written by the prophet Muhammad. After Jesus was cruci-fied for calling himself the Christ, the promised Jewish Messiah, his followers began to pull further away from their Jewish roots. They based their beliefs on what became called the New Testa-ment of teachings from Jesus and his disciples, and they reached out to Jews and non-Jews (Gentiles) to teach them these beliefs. It may seem with this brief historical overview that the Mono-theistic Faith worldview does not have much in common at all across its three primary constituents. However, all three share the beliefs outlined here.

Source. Each of these religions adheres to a set of sacred writings that provide the foundation for their beliefs. They believe that these scriptures were inspired by the Supreme Being and given to humans to capture in written form and to use as the basis for directing human behavior. Each also claims Abraham as the original father of the religion. In the scriptural story, Abraham was called by God/Jehovah/Allah to be the father of a great nation and was told that he and his wife, Sarah, would have offspring even though they were both quite aged and had been unable to conceive. After his calling, Abraham fathered a son, Ishmael, with a servant woman, and a second son, Isaac, with his wife, Sarah. Muslims claim Ishmael—the first child—as the son promised by Allah, but Jews and Christians claim Isaac—the one born of Sarah—as the promised son. It is this difference of belief that initiates the separate paths of the three monotheistic religions.

Philosophy. All three believe in a Supreme Being creator who transcends this world, who provides for the needs of human beings, and who sits in judgment of them. Adherents believe in moral absolutes for right and wrong behavior, that the sacred writings are the source of all true wisdom, and that humans are the Supreme Being's highest creation. All three believe in the existence of Heaven, where the faithful go, and in Hell, where the rest are punished for eternity. They all emphasize the importance of relationship with God/Allah/Jehovah through prayer, including prayers of thanksgiving, forgiveness, and provision. They emphasize a dependence on the Supreme Being for direction and meaning in life, for sustenance and provision, and for peace that transcends their own capacity to create or understand. God/Allah/Jehovah created the heavens and the earth, all people, animals, and vegetation, as well as all living organisms.

Psychology. Human beings have choice and free will as gifts from the Supreme Being, but often make poor decisions that draw them away from correct behavior and put a wedge between themselves and God/Allah/Jehovah. This is called "sin," and human beings have an innate tendency to engage in it. The evidence for this innate tendency exists in the self-focused, self-gratifying, vengeful, and jealous behaviors we human beings seem to exhibit. While the Supreme Being is apart from people and outside their human bodies, if they believe in him, his spirit resides within them in the form of a conscience that warns them when they are about to engage in wrong behavior and makes them feel guilty if they transgress. People have been given free will by their Creator and should, therefore, make choices that are selfless and consistent with the Creator's will. Mental health is the result of clearly focusing on the Supreme Being, changing selfish behaviors that distance us from him, and turning burdens, cares, and worries over to him through prayer.

Sociology. Other people either encourage right behavior or support wrong behavior that is contrary to the Supreme Being's laws and precepts. Right behavior is consistent with the Creator's will, and includes things like feeding the hungry, clothing the naked, and protecting the vulnerable. It also includes being honest with people, expressing compassion, helping in times of need, and other acts of kindness. Wrong behavior includes things like stealing, cheating, deliberately hurting others, lying, and being envious of their possessions. Engaging with others in prayer and worship is important in keeping one's focus on righteous things. The presence of evil in the world, in the form of Satan (Lucifer), takes people's innate tendency to sin and exaggerates it so that they engage in even worse behavior.

People's hurtful behavior is the result of pulling so far from the Supreme Being that their hearts have become hardened and they cannot perceive the reality of the pain they have inflicted on others. One must be part of a congregation of believers in order to resist Satan's influences and one's own selfish drives, and to help protect others in their group and in the world from these influences. In addition to worship and prayer, congregations typically encourage learning from the sacred words of God/Jehovah/Allah and the prophets through classes and programs.

Truth. Bottom line, the Truth is that which is written in the sacred books and scriptures, and it rests on the Word of God/Jehovah/Allah. If it does not come from the heart and mind of this Supreme Being, it is not Truth. Truth is known or discerned with the help of the Supreme Being; the closer people draw to God and the more they lean on him, the greater their wisdom about the Truth.

NEW AGE MYSTICISM. Though the term "new age" is of fairly recent vintage, the origin of this worldview is quite ancient and starts with Hinduism in India. The earliest form of mysticism, in the form of Brahmanism, started about 3,000 years ago. Mysticism is the belief that direct knowledge of spiritual truth or ultimate reality can be attained through a high level of enlightenment, intuition, or insight that is qualitatively different from typical perception via the senses. Most often, such enlightenment is achieved through meditation, prayer, ceremonies, drugs, or subjecting the physical body to hardship such as fasting. It was just such an experience that Siddhartha Gautama experienced centuries later in India after embarking on a solitary quest for peace and enlightenment. He became known as Buddha—one who has found enlightenment—and his teachings were written down after his death to form the basis of Buddhism.

Still later, other forms of this worldview were born, including Zen Buddhism, Confucianism, Taoism, and Shintoism. In many native populations across the globe, similar enlightenment experiences came to be popular. Like Hinduism, Buddhism, and other Eastern religions, New Age believes in altering one's consciousness in order to achieve a form of greater enlightenment. Most New Age focus can be characterized as a form of spirituality aimed at providing an alternative to the dominant Judeo-Christian religion. The name New Age was popularized by American mass media during the late 1980s to describe adherents who were involved in meditation, psychic experiences, holistic and alternative health, and other such practices.

Source. The initial source of mysticism came from the Eastern religions, as noted above. Some of these religions have sacred scriptures, some do not. The primary Hindu writings include the Upanishads and the Vedas, as well as the later work entitled, Bhagavad-Gita, which was first published in English in 1785. The New Age movement traces its roots from these earliest mystic experiences, but is founded more intentionally on 18th and 19th century philosophers and writers such as Goethe, Nietzsche, Baudelaire, Emerson, and de Balzac.

Philosophy. New Age does not espouse specific practices or scriptures, but has a foundational belief in a universal consciousness that connects all humans, as well as faith in Nature, and a broad sense of the divine. Instead of mimicking organized religions, New Age adherents tend to construct their own spiritual beliefs based on the mystic traditions noted above, as well as shamanism and occultism. In the mystic tradition, only immediate, direct knowledge taken into a person's consciousness and deep understanding of the meaning behind what the person perceives are valid. The mystic's aim is to move from beliefs and observations to deeper knowledge and meaning—into a transcendent experience that goes beyond the self and that connects to a universal life force or spirit.

The core beliefs of most new age mystic adherents include the notion that all life in the universe is spiritually interconnected via the same universal energy source. Death is not considered the end, but rather life in a different form of being as in reincarnation. Further, they believe that all religions share a mystical core of truth and that the Judeo-Christian writings contain important truths, but that many other truths are not found there. Everything is seen to have spiritual meaning and lessons to be learned, with no coincidences or accidents. We are meant to be here on this Earth, and we are always exactly where we need to be to learn from the situation that confronts us. There are many spiritual paths and there is no one religious doctrine that is the best path to follow.

Psychology. Like postmodernism, the New Age Mysticism worldview emphasizes the importance of subjective knowledge and individual choice in a situation, and places a higher value on personal intuition over someone else's "expert opinion." They believe the human mind has vast powers that are capable of creating one's own reality, and that individuals each have a purpose on Earth that is related to learning lessons about love and other basic truths. Increasing wisdom, willpower, and communion with the universe necessitates removing any sensory, feeling, or thought illusions that get in the way. The process of "becoming" is a central one to New Age Mystical psychology, and it is essentially an unfolding process that requires experiences and reflection to reach a deep sense of who you are and how you achieve knowing. Adherents believe that dreams and psychic experiences are avenues through which their souls express themselves.

Sociology. New Age is a values-based, sociopolitical movement that offers a broad and deep menu of ideas and practices from which people select their own preferred approach with which to identify. Meditation, yoga, and other Eastern practices are seen as valuable and are often supported by groups and group-based activities. Science and spirituality are viewed as harmonious, so that new discoveries in science will move people to a deeper understanding of spiritual principles. Connecting and interconnecting are very important, and they occur in relationships with others, with Mother Earth/environment, and with a higher power/god. New Age Mystics connect with each other through lectures and fairs, products such as books, music, crystals, or incense, and the utilization of spiritual directors, healers, and fortune-tellers.

Truth. For New Age Mysticism adherents, the truth is relative and is akin to the Vedic belief in "one truth, but many paths," or the Zen Buddhist philosophy of "many paths, one mountain." This approach to truth states that truth itself is defined by each individual and his or her personal experience of it, and it is based on personal choice in the matter.

NATURALISTIC HUMANISM. This philosophy is based on the assumption that the universe and nature are all that exist, and Naturalistic Humanists seek to understand the universe through science and its methodology of critical inquiry. Such inquiry is based on the use of logical analysis and empirical evidence to generate reliable conclusions and knowledge. Naturalistic Humanism holds that the universe has developed over a long and complex evolutionary process via the immutable laws of nature, and that the cosmos is all that there was, is, or ever will be. There is a preference for free inquiry over established doctrine, of scientific method over revealed wisdom and theistic morality. In short, Naturalistic Humanists believe that humans have ultimate value and can remedy their own societal problems, and that there is nothing supernatural in the creation or maintenance of the universe. A key thread throughout this philosophy is rational skepticism—withholding belief where there is no clear evidence and only believing what is supported by the available evidence that can be studied and understood by scientific methods.

Source. Naturalistic Humanism is an ethical, scientific philosophy that traces its roots back to the philosophers and poets of ancient Greece and Rome, as well as to Confucian China and the Charvaka movement in India. For the last 500 years, humanistic writers, scientists, and thinkers have been expressing a renewed emphasis on the power of human beings to solve their own problems and conquer uncharted frontiers. Philosophers from Francis Bacon to John Dewey have emphasized the power over nature that scientific method and knowledge offers, and how these findings can contribute immeasurably to human advancement and happiness.

In 1846, George Jacob Holyoke used the term "secularism" to describe a form of opinion that concerns itself solely with questions and issues that can be tested by life experiences. The earliest use of the term "secular humanism" was by Supreme Court Justice Hugo Black, who in 1961 lumped humanism into the category of religions that do not teach a belief in the existence of God. Special days on the humanist calendar include the summer and winter solstices, as well as Charles Darwin's birthday.

Philosophy. Holding a deep belief that humanity must take responsibility for its own destiny, Naturalistic Humanists assert that moral values are properly founded on human nature and experience alone. Non-theistic in their beliefs, adherents hold to the notion that there is no evidence that a supernatural power has ever needed or wanted anything from humans, has ever communicated with them, or has ever interfered with the laws of nature to either help or punish anyone. Therefore, since there is no known and accepted empirical knowledge supporting the existence of a god, then a supernatural power does not exist.

Naturalistic Humanism has nothing to do with spiritual, religions, or ecclesiastical doctrines, beliefs, or hierarchies—it considers all forms of the supernatural to be myth. Moral values stem from people's experiences, ethics come from human needs and interests, and the purpose of life is what people make it to be. Adherents believe that humans have evolved as a product of Nature, that the mind is not separate from the physical brain, and that there can be no conscious survival of spirit after death since body and personality are inseparable. The use of reason and cognition enables humans to make wiser choices and to appraise ethical values in the light of the observable evidence and consequences.

Psychology. The focus of Naturalistic Humanism is on using human effort to meet their own needs and the belief that such efforts are most effective when they combine scientific method and compassion for fellow human beings. Humans have the power and potential to solve their own problems through science and reason, they possess genuine freedom of creative choice—within certain limits—and they shape their own future and destiny. People find their purpose in life and maximize their life satisfaction by developing their talents and using them in the service of humanity. Affirming the dignity of each human being, this philosophy upholds the maximization of individual liberty and opportunity within the limits of socially responsible behavior. Goals in life stem from human needs and interests, rather than from supernatural sources; consequently, humanity must take responsibility for its own destiny.

Sociology. Standing for human rights and social justice, Naturalistic Humanists believe that this is the only life of which we have certain knowledge, and that, therefore, we must make it the best possible life for ourselves and others around us. All human beings must seek a reason for their existence within the boundaries of our physical world, and that reason is heavily influenced by the imperative to love others and to provide selfless service to them. More specifically, the emphasis here is on improving equity and stability, alleviating poverty, reducing conflict, and safeguarding the environment. Although many societal and world problems seem intractable, Naturalistic Humanists believe that talents and resources can be marshaled and that better lives can be attained incrementally by members of the human community. They hold that individuals attain the good life by inter-weaving their own personal satisfactions and self-development with activities that contribute significantly to the community's welfare.

Truth. In accordance with its emphasis on scientific method, Naturalistic Humanism believes that truth lies in the continuous questioning of basic assumptions and convictions, and that it evolves through experimental testing, new facts, and rigorous reasoning. Since human beings possess the freedom and capacity to make creative choices and take action, they determine their own truth and their own destiny. Consequently, truth is a relative and evolving entity that changes as new scientific evidence or life experience informs it. There are no absolute truths to the Naturalistic Humanist. There exist a variety of truths, but only one source of reliable knowledge about the natural world, which is the scientific method based on empirical evidence and logical reasoning.

As we look across these three worldviews and understand their basic tenets and how these impact individuals and groups, we see three fairly distinct origins, beliefs, and practices. Perhaps most distinct is how these three approach the concept of truth. For the Monotheistic Faiths, the truth is absolute and is based on sacred writings that capture the perspective of the one and only Supreme Being. For New Age Mystics, the truth is personal and subjective—a transcendent experience that goes beyond the self and that connects to a deeper, universal flow of truth. Naturalist Humanists view the truth from a totally empirical point of view. In their minds, truth is an evolving concept that is tested by scientific method and verified by each individual as his or her own truth. In the next chapter, we will discuss how to create Bedrock Truth that will eventually overcome the anchor lie to which you have held firmly throughout your life.

REFLECTION MOMENT—QUESTIONS TO CONSIDER

Take some time now to thoughtfully consider your answers to these questions, and capture them here or write them on a separate sheet of paper. You can use your responses to focus your thinking and to share with others in a discussion group based on this book.

1. Of the three worldviews described—Monotheistic Faith, New Age Mysticism, or Naturalistic Humanism—which one, or combination, best describes your own worldview?

2. Of the competing worldviews (other than the one you chose for question number 1, above) which aspects of their philosophy, psychology, or sociology most appeal to you?

3. How important do you think it is to believe in one particular worldview and to have your thinking aligned to it, versus developing your own more eclectic approach that picks and chooses from all three?

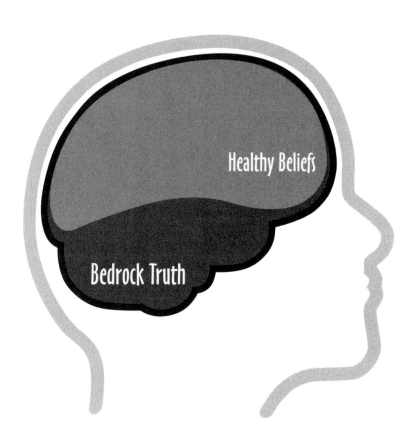

9

Your Bedrock Truth

When I first discovered the idea that my beliefs about truth and other fundamental questions in life were informed by my worldview, I was rather surprised. I had learned about different philosophies and religions in the past, but it had not occurred to me that differences in religious practices were actually reflective of a basic worldview that colored every aspect of a person's life. Perhaps you have also been somewhat in the dark about the depth and breadth of the fabric of your own worldview. Hopefully, the previous chapter helped you shed light on your worldview, so that you are more fully informed about its origins and how the component parts fit together philosophically.

This chapter is designed to help you think through the question, "What is the bedrock truth that counter-balances the anchor lie in my life?" In order to completely benefit from this section, you will need to have thought through and identified your anchor lie in previous chapters. As we discussed there, the basic lie that you have held onto since early childhood focuses on your acceptability in others' eyes. Unconscious and irrational, this lie is lodged in the emotional memory part of your brain and makes it nearly impossible to engage in high performance responses to situations once it gets aroused inside you. Your lie keeps whispering in your internal ear that you are not lovable, not competent, not worthy, not able to be forgiven, that nothing good will ever happen for you, or no one understands or wants to get to know you.

I call this the anchor lie because it firmly holds fears and faulty beliefs inside you and makes it very difficult to recognize them and get past them. Difficult, but not impossible. The key is to believe and accept the idea that your anchor lie is not true and to replace it with your bedrock truth. The purpose of the previous chapter was to help you determine how your beliefs are founded and what you recognize to be true from your world-view. Now, we will take that perspective and use it to think through the bedrock truth in your life.

To distill it down for you, there are three seminal paths to determining your own **Bedrock Truth:**

Supreme Being—your Truth is reflected in what you know to be true from the God/Jehovah/Allah perspective through sacred writings and prayer. You are wondrously made by the Creator of the universe, and this Supreme Being would not make you in a way that is unacceptable to others. Truth is absolute, it does not change nor waver.

Personal Intuition—your truth is defined by yourself and your personal experience of it, and you have a choice in the matter. Your path to this truth is directed by you, and the spiritual experiences you choose to encounter on the way will provide you with the capacity to tap into a universal life force so that you can know the truth about you. Truth is subjective and intuitive, not at all absolute.

Empirical Evidence—you determine what is true for you through continuous questioning of basic assumptions and convictions. Your truth will evolve through the new facts you encounter and the rigorous reasoning you employ to figure it out. You have the freedom and capacity to make creative choices; consequently, you determine your own truth. There is no absolute Truth, but rather a variety of truths based on empirical evidence and logical reasoning.

In my work coaching clients, we have talked about discerning their bedrock truth through these same three pathways. Some of my clients have a strong monotheistic faith and lean on it to determine that the Truth is "God loves me; therefore, I am totally acceptable." In many ways, it is easiest to work with these clients because they believe in a Supreme Being whose power is greater than their own and they simply trust in that. Whenever they feel their early warning of thoughtless reaction to a situation, they say a brief prayer, turn the situation over to God/Allah/Jehovah, and remind themselves of the Truth. Sometimes, the fear state seems much more real and powerful than does the presence of the Supreme Being in a situation and they have difficulty experiencing the Truth from a higher perspective, even though they believe it to be so.

Others rely on their subjective experience of the truth and just know that, for example, "I'm an intelligent, interesting, and valued person." They feel this to be true in their hearts and to the very core of their being. It is not necessary for them to cite evidence for this conclusion or lean on the idea of a Supreme Being. Instead, they have an intuitive sense that it is true and they operate accordingly. When they begin to react and exhibit a retroaction or two, they deliberately get re-centered and remind themselves of their bedrock truth. Since this is based on what most people experience as a type of feeling state, it is sometimes more difficult for these people to break out of a fear reaction. They feel the fear strongly and it tends to mask their capacity to quickly change to an opposite feeling state.

Still others look at how their friends, family, and coworkers see them and conclude something like, "I am a person of integrity, consistency, and reliability." They literally use the evidence of people in their work and non-work circles to help them determine their bedrock truth. In addition, they use their own observations of themselves (video tapes, photos, audio tapes, etc.) to come to a conclusion about the truth. As new evidence comes in or as their behaviors change in a deliberate effort like coaching, they re-calibrate the bedrock truth for themselves.

The complication these people encounter is that sometimes the evidence is contrary across the sources being tapped, and other times it runs directly counter to what they believe the bedrock truth to be. For example, how can a person who believes in empirical evidence determine the truth when he sees himself as a person of integrity, consistency, and reliability, but his wife or boss or teenage children see him as the opposite? Where, then, is the empirical truth? And if the bedrock truth is a continually evolving process based on evidence, how do you make sure you are recalibrating often enough to ascertain the current state of truth?

Your bedrock truth can be fully formulated in one of these three paths, or you may choose to create your own version of the truth about you by combining worldviews. The critical component of your truth is that it is compelling enough to be an unshakable, unwavering bedrock support for you when your fears and faulty beliefs get stirred up by circumstances around you. In these moments, a relative or half-baked truth will not do. A truth that you are unsure of or hesitant about will not suffice. You must know with every fiber of your being that what you believe to be true about you—your bedrock truth—is true indeed. It is essential that your head, heart, and gut are aligned in their acceptance and recognition of this truth. Otherwise, the anchor lie will pull you back down and your fears and faulty beliefs will take over again as you engage in your visible retroactions.

Knowing your bedrock truth also provides a foundation for your healthy beliefs. Like the faulty beliefs you desire to replace, healthy ones are based on something powerful and compelling. Your faulty beliefs are based on the anchor lie, which can be very compelling; healthy beliefs must be anchored on a truth which is even more palpable and motivating to you. Having a strong hold on this truth gives you a firm stepping-off place from which to engage in your healthy beliefs and eventually replace the faulty beliefs you have carried throughout your life.

REFLECTION MOMENT—QUESTIONS TO CONSIDER

Take some time now to thoughtfully consider your answers to these questions, and capture them here or write them on a separate sheet of paper. You can use your responses to focus your thinking and to share with others in a discussion group based on this book.

1. What is the Bedrock Truth about You?

2. In what way does your Bedrock Truth help support the new, healthy beliefs that you have identified and are motivated to use in your life?

3. What do you think your biggest obstacle will be in consistently behaving based on your Bedrock Truth and healthy beliefs?

AFTERWORD

In my garage, up on a dusty shelf where I seldom dig, sits an old two-person mountain tent that I bought 30 years ago. Inside the life story of that tent lies an allegory for the effects of anchor lies, irrational fears, and faulty beliefs in your life. Perhaps you have had a similar experience that can provide you with a powerful illustration of these influences.

My parents and brothers and I went camping every year in July for our vacation, and I knew it was important to have a good tent that would not leak and that could last forever if you took proper care of it. I was so proud of my little tent because it was constructed of sturdy, heavy-weight canvas and it had heavy-duty zippers on the front screen and on the little window in the back. Clearly, it was one that could stand up to a lifetime or more of wear. More important in some ways was the color— a golden, wheat-colored yellow that stood out among the more dour greens and browns of typical tents in those days.

Several years after I bought the tent, a friend borrowed it to go camping with another person. Before she could take the tent, however, I made my friend listen to a lengthy tutorial on how to set it up properly, how to keep it swept clean using the special hand broom passed down to me from my parents, and how to fold it perfectly to fit into the small canvas carrying bag. With everything in order, I released her with the tent and wished her a safe and fun trip.

When she returned, she handed me the tent neatly folded and packed inside the carrying bag and thanked me for letting her use it. Without thinking, I simply put the tent in a storage area and did not open it up to check on its condition. Because of lots of other activities in my life at the time, I did not actually open up the tent again for a couple of years.

When I did finally open up the canvas carrying bag and pull out my lovely yellow tent, the first thing I noticed was the smell. It reminded me of the basement of the house in which I spent my early childhood. This was the kind of basement that had one window and a door, but was mostly very dark and dank. The stale, musty smell that greeted my nostrils as I gingerly unfolded my tent brought me back to playing hide and seek among the spider webs in that basement. I spread the tent out on the ground, slipped inside the unzipped front entrance, and then put in the poles on both ends to open it up. That's when I first noticed it.

"It" was a large, greenish-black stain the size of a jack-o-lantern that was now staring at me tauntingly from the golden, wheat-yellow exterior of the tent. Having never seen or smelled mildew close up before, I was not sure exactly what it was. But soon it became clear that the tent was probably packed in a damp condition a couple of years earlier, and I had failed to open it up to make sure it was ready to be stored for a while. I wanted to blame my friend for despoiling this beautiful yellow tent, but knew inside that it was my fault for not making sure it was totally dry. Grieving just a little for my tent, I opened it up fully and staked it out in the bright July sunshine to let it sit for several days. In the course of those days, the smell totally went away and the stain greatly reduced in size and color. However, it never totally disappeared and is still there today, up on the shelf in my garage.

What's the point of this sentimental story? It perfectly illustrates the process on which you have embarked by beginning to deal with your anchor lies and irrational fears. The mildew stain is symbolic of your anchor lie and the fears and faulty beliefs that support it. Somehow, that stain got there on the perfect yellow tent of your early childhood. It does not belong there, was not a part of the original fabric of your being, but now it sits there and will not go away on its own. You can never totally remove it, but you can decrease the ugly impact of it on your life. Instead of bright, summer sunshine, you have the intensity of your newfound healthy beliefs and bedrock truth to dry out the stain and make it begin to fade away. The longer you expose those anchor lies and faulty beliefs to the healing power of your bedrock truth and healthy beliefs, the smaller and less intense your mildew stain will become.

Over time, your stain will have almost no lasting negative effects on your life. When those rare occasions occur where the fears and faulty beliefs get stirred up again, you will quickly and effectively shine the light of truth on them and move on in a highly effective manner. At some point when these truths and healthy beliefs have bleached out your mildew stain to a light enough shade, you will begin to see the mildew stains of others around you. You will recognize their retroactions as they engage in them and you will look at them with compassion, knowing that you also have such a mildew stain, and that you can help these others shine a little truth on their fears and faulty beliefs.

Who knows—perhaps at some point in your life, you will become a source of light that draws people like a beacon. I hope this book has helped you get past the stain to see the truth about you, and that truth will begin to set you free. Perhaps you will devote some part of your life to helping others recognize the effects of their stain and giving them the hope and the tools to bleach it out in the light of truth. May it be so in your lifetime.

GLOSSARY

Anchor Lies—these irrational, unconscious lies tell us in what way we are fundamentally unacceptable to others. They can be distilled down to five primary lies, though you may believe a combination of more than one:

- **Abandonment**—"I will never experience love, nobody cares about me or accepts me; I am alone, not lovable."

- **Shamefulness**—"I am nobody, and I need to hide who I am; I can never be forgiven; I will always be tainted, will never amount to anything; I don't deserve the acceptance of others."

- **Invalidation**—"I'm too weak or stupid to do anything right; I cannot do anything on my own; I am not worthy or important, not respected in any way."

- **Hopelessness**—"I will never be happy or whole in my life; nothing good will ever happen for me, and I cannot trust anyone to help me."

- **Alienation**—"I'm different from the others, standing alone; I'm weird, odd, or strange in their eyes; no one understands me or wants to get to know me."

Each one of them represents a belief aimed at your core self and each supports the underlying conclusion, "There's something wrong with me."

Bedrock Truth—that deeply-held belief about who you are at the very core of your being, and how acceptable that core person is to others. It is bedrock because it provides the foundation for functioning in a healthier, more effective way—not hindered by your anchor lie, faulty beliefs, or irrational fears. It is truth because it is based on how you see yourself as a rational adult and how your worldview informs your thinking in the matter. For the Monotheistic Faiths, the truth is absolute and is based on sacred writings that capture the perspective of the one and only Supreme Being. For New Age Mystics, the truth is personal and subjective—a transcendent experience that goes beyond the self and that connects to a deeper, universal flow of truth. Naturalist Humanists view the truth from a totally empirical point of view. In their minds, truth is an evolving concept that is tested by scientific method and verified by each individual as his or her own truth.

Cortex—the part of the brain in which logical analysis, creative problem solving, memory, and other complicated conscious functions operate.

Faulty Beliefs—can be thought of as "if, then" statements that start with a belief and end with a faulty promise of protection. These kinds of beliefs are faulty for two major reasons. First, they have their origin in early childhood, well before one is capable of logical analysis. Since they began before logic, they are illogical or irrational in nature. The promise held within such faulty beliefs is always naïve and simplistic—and almost never true. Second, they have become unconscious over the years so that we are not aware in our cortexes that we are thinking them, but nonetheless, they give direction to our behavior. When they combine with one of the three fundamental irrational fears, they result in thoughtless behaviors called retroactions. We develop faulty beliefs to protect ourselves from harm, but usually end up just getting in the way of our own effectiveness.

Healthy Beliefs—are conscious, rational beliefs that can be used to motivate and guide high performance behaviors at work, at home, and in your community. These beliefs do not direct you to stuff feelings or to use affirmations to try to change behaviors, but instead help bring into your conscious mind the realization of what is happening under the surface with your unconscious, irrational fears, faulty beliefs, and anchor lie. You can use these conscious beliefs to reaffirm the truth of each situation you face and to guide your subsequent behavior through a healthy, high performance attitude. As you develop healthy beliefs to replace the faulty beliefs you have lived with all your life, they must be more than hollow affirmations of who you want to become. They must be believable and sustainable, and they must reflect who you are at the very core of your personality.

Irrational Fears—the three most fundamental irrational fears that get stirred up inside you and undermine your sense of well-being are these (usually one is more powerful for you than the others):

- **Personal rejection.** People will not like me, accept me, or include me.
- **Role insignificance.** Others in authority will not look to me, value me, or allow me to play an important role.
- **Irreparable hurt.** The situation will shift dramatically and people important to me or I, myself, will be damaged emotionally, financially, or physically.

These fears have their origin in moments of upset from early childhood, well before you are capable of logical analysis. When they combine with a faulty belief, they result in thoughtless behaviors called retroactions.

Limbic System—these brain components—located between the cortex and the brain stem—store memories that are primarily emotional in nature. Our irrational fears, faulty beliefs, and anchor lie(s) are embedded in this part of the brain. Our retroactions start to occur when our left brain cortex explanations and information do not fit with our right brain limbic system experiences and feelings.

Needs—as human beings, we have several fundamental needs that must be met in order for us to feel fulfilled. The three most basic needs can be thought of as respect, acceptance, and security. We need to know that we are respected—important,

significant, valued, worthy—in our work and in our relationships. We need to feel accepted in these areas as well—to know
that we are liked, loved, and included. Finally, we need to know
that we will be secure from emotional, physical, financial, or
interpersonal harm.

Reaction—something you do when, for example, your hand
touches a hot stovetop. Your central nervous system reflexively
sends an electronic impulse to your hand/arm muscles to pull
back immediately in a "reflex arc" reaction. The result is a swift
and "thoughtless" behavior that protects your flesh from severe
burns. When your underlying irrational fears or anchor lie
become stirred up as a result of something that happens around
you, your limbic system reacts in a similar way. (See retroaction.)

Response—something that happens when you take in information through your senses—sight, smell, touch, taste, audition—
and consider it within the cortex of your brain before speaking
or acting. When you deliver a carefully considered response
to a stimulus, you must draw upon your intellect, values, emotions, and previous experiences. Most of the decisions you make
at work or at home are generated by this kind of considered
response.

Retroactions—are reflexive behaviors you exhibit in the present, but that are actually reacting to some occurrence or series
of occurrences from your past. These automatic reactions echo
fears and faulty beliefs from your early childhood and, in some
ways, represent a regression to more childish behavior. When

your irrational fear of personal rejection, role insignificance, or irreparable harm instantaneously connects with a faulty belief in your subconscious mind, you begin to behave in a way that can best be characterized as a thoughtless reaction, or retroaction. They are intended to protect you from these irrational fears, but instead they make your thoughtless reactions even more obvious to the people around you. Typical retroactions are confusion, perfectionism, defensiveness, resistance, and discouragement. These five retroactions represent the "tip of the iceberg" of our thoughtless reactions—the part we can visibly observe in others and they can see in us.

Worldview—the way you make sense of philosophy, psychology, and sociology, as well as the vehicle through which you define truth. There are three primary worldviews today—Monotheistic Faith, Naturalistic Humanism, and New Age Mysticism. Monotheistic Faith is clearly a religious worldview, based on the teachings of the Judeo-Christian and Islamic faiths, and it is part of the foundational fabric of North and South America, Europe, the Middle East, and various other countries around the world. Naturalistic Humanism is a religious-like worldview that believes in Nature rather than God/Allah/Jehovah, and that focuses on the role of self-actualization and social institutions in a person's development. New Age Mysticism holds that god exists in all things and there is a collective consciousness. Core to this worldview is the belief that personal growth requires connecting to the god within ourselves.

ABOUT THE AUTHOR

Bruce E. Roselle, PhD, is a psychologist who helps organizations hire and develop great leaders. For more than 20 years, he has supported organizations in the areas of leadership and team development, executive coaching, and psychological assessment. Bringing a breadth of experience and a deep sense of purpose to his work, Bruce helps organizational leaders develop greater effectiveness and a more wholehearted, fearless attitude toward their work. He has served companies ranging from high-tech and manufacturing to service firms, as well as non-profit organizations, public institutions, and churches.

His first book, *Vital Truths: the secret to living and leading wholeheartedly,* was published by Beaver's Pond Press in 2002. He has written and co-written articles that appeared in *Counseling and Human Development,* the Executive Excellence magazine, and the *Career Development Quarterly.* In addition, he has been quoted in newspapers, magazines, radio and television on his views regarding the impact of fears and faulty beliefs, as well as creating work that is fun, dealing with stress at work, identifying personality characteristics that make individuals more hirable, and leading wholeheartedly.

A member of the American Society for Training and Development and the American Association of Christian Counselors, Bruce is past president of the Minnesota Career Development Association, and has served on its Board of Directors. This organization awarded him the Jules Kerlan Outstanding Achievement Award in 2003 for his significant contributions in the field of career guidance, counseling, and development. He holds Doctor of Philosophy and Master of Arts degrees in Educational Psychology/Counseling from the University of Minnesota. He earned his Bachelor of Arts degree in Psychology from Northwestern University.

Bruce lives in the Twin Cities with his wife, Cindy, and has two grown children. Recognizing that the true root of fearless leadership in his life lies in his relationship with God, he is committed to Monotheistic Faith as the worldview that provides the foundation for his work and family life. When asked, he openly acknowledges that without the central presence of God in his life, his work and relationships would be half-hearted at best. He can be reached by phone at 763-712-0086 or by email at **roselleleadership.com** (click on Contact Us).

Other LEADER PRESS publications by Bruce E. Roselle, PhD, available through www.roselleleadership.com:

FULLVIEW Feedback Inventory™, an online, multi-rater feedback inventory for assessing the strengths and development needs of managers and executives.

Handbook for Fearless Leaders, a resource book of effective management and leadership techniques to support executive coaching.

Vital Truths, the secret to living and leading wholeheartedly, Beaver's Pond Press, Edina, MN (2002).

Wholehearted Leadership: Helping Good Managers Become Great Leaders, a set of training materials to support 12 two-hour training sessions that match the 12 core competencies measured in the FULLVIEW Feedback Inventory™.

LEADER PRESS

is the publication division of Roselle Leadership Strategies, Inc. The philosophy at Roselle Leadership Strategies (RLS) is that it takes great leaders to develop engaged employees and committed customers/clients in a way that makes a difference to an organization's bottom line.

Through psychological assessments, RLS helps organizations hire candidates who have the potential to become great leaders, and assists them in identifying and growing high potential leaders.

Once managers and executives are on board and in the right positions, RLS provides individualized executive coaching, custom leadership development training, and team-building for management groups or entire departments. The approach emphasizes the importance of functioning effectively as whole-hearted, fearless leaders.

The starting point for management or executive development often is RLS's proprietary FULLVIEW Feedback Inventory™, a multi-rater, 360-degree instrument that identifies strengths to leverage as well as potential career derailers to overcome.